TANKMASTER

A practical guide to setting up your

TROPICAL
FRESHWATER AQUARIUM

GINA SANDFORD

BARRON'S

CREDITS AND CONTENTS

Author

Gina Sandford's interest in fishkeeping began with a goldfish and developed to include sticklebacks, young perch, pike, and eventually tropical fish. She has kept and bred many species, but has a particular interest in catfishes. She has written several books and contributed many articles to magazines and journals. Gina travels widely, giving audiovisual presentations and lectures to both experienced and young audiences.

Credits

Created and designed: Ideas into Print,
New Ash Green, Kent DA3 8JD, England.

First edition for the United States and Canada published in 2000 by Barron's Educational Series, Inc.
First published in 1999 by Interpet Publishing
Original edition © 1999 by Interpet Publishing

All inquiries should be addressed to:
Barron's Educational Series, Inc.
250 Wireless Boulevard
Hauppauge, New York 11788
http://www.barronseduc.com

International Standard Book No. 0-7641-5266-1
Library of Congress Catalog Card No. 99-68532

Printed in China
9 8 7 6 5 4 3 2 1

Below: Once your tank has become well established, you can add a small school of colorful neon tetras (Paracheirodon innesi). Make sure there are no other fish in the aquarium large enough to eat them.

Contents

Part One: Setting up the aquarium 6-41

Choosing a tank and stand	8
Placing the tank	10
Installing the tank	12
Choosing and preparing substrates	14
Choosing an internal power filter	16
Heating the water	18
Choosing and preparing wood	20
Choosing and cleaning rocks	22
Adding the water	24
Running the system before adding plants	26
Planting the aquarium	28
Preparing the hood	34
Fitting the condensation tray and hood	36
Choosing a background and maturing the tank	38
Adding the fish	40

Part Two: Options and continuing care 43-75

Using an external power filter	44
Undergravel and other types of filters	46
Other types of tank decoration	48
A selection of tropical aquarium plants	50
Using plastic plants in the aquarium	54
A selection of fish for your first aquarium	56
Foods and feeding	62
Breeding your fish	64
Health care	66
Regular maintenance	70
Index and credits	76

For a peaceful aquarium, keep tiger barbs (Barbus tetrazona) in a school.

Setting up the aquarium

Aimed at complete novices, the purpose of this book is to take the worry out of setting up your first aquarium. In the first part we show how to set up the aquarium. It is important to realize that there are choices to be made at each stage, as the products available vary around the world. However, the principles of setting up and operating remain the same. This is particularly important when it comes to the filtration and lighting sections, as electrical safety standards and their implementation differ from country to country and this will affect the products available. We demonstrate a setup that takes into account ease of operation and cost efficiency, so that even children on a small weekly allowance should be able to keep fish. In the second part we discuss the alternative equipment, plants, and fish, and examine what happens when you put everything together. We suggest that you read the book through first before you buy any equipment, so that you have a good understanding of what you need, where to put it, how it goes together, and where you can buy it.

Finding a reliable aquatic retailer is the key. What you need is a dedicated aquatic outlet. Look at several before you pick one. Listen to the advice you are offered and look at the health of the livestock. See how long people stay in the stop; fishkeepers are notorious for spending several hours in a good establishment looking around and talking with the staff. Everyone has to start somewhere and a good aquatic dealer will be aware that novices are potential customers for a long time if they are treated properly. Visit the shop when it is quiet, say during the week or when it first opens in the morning, so that the retailer can guide you through the products to determine which ones are right for your needs. When you come to buy your tropical freshwater fish, do not be put off if the retailer will not sell you a certain creature because it grows too large, has a bad temper, will not agree with your other fish, or is difficult to feed.

Your next task is to put your purchases together to create your aquarium. Over the next pages we will take you through the process step by step. Take your time over this; it is not a race. The aim is to complete each step successfully so that by the end, you will have a fully working aquarium to house and display tropical freshwater fish and plants in a healthy and attractive environment. Above all, enjoy your first venture into this fascinating hobby.

Tank and stand or cabinet styles are very much a matter of personal taste and there is a wide range of designs to choose from. Your main considerations should be: the available space in your home; how much you want to spend, the number and size of fish you want to keep, which in turn will be governed by surface area (see page 26), and how you are going to transport the tank and stand home.

Tanks are normally rectangular and constructed of glass sheets bonded together with silicone sealant. Retailers carry the standard sizes, but customized sizes can be made to order. If you take this route, remember that your cabinet or stand will also need to be custom-made. Some tanks are supplied complete with hoods. They are either the standard shape that we will demonstrate in this book or an integral hood. The choice is yours.

Good-quality aquatic outlets will advise you on the best choices within your price range and many will offer to deliver bulky items that will not fit into your car, but some may charge for this extra service.

Acrylic tanks

Acrylic tanks are usually more expensive, but are becoming a popular alternative to glass. They are a great improvement on the old-style plastic aquariums that scratched and stained easily.

Tanks are heavy

Given the weight of a furnished aquarium full of water, you are strongly advised not to use an existing piece of furniture as a stand. It will not have been constructed to support such a heavy weight and could collapse.

Below: *The majority of available metal aquarium stands are of one-piece construction and are ready for the tank to be set in place. Some wooden stands may require assembly, but this is often done by the seller.*

Standard tank sizes

You can buy all-glass aquariums in a range of standard sizes, in combinations of the following dimensions:

Length: *60, 90, or 120 cm (24, 36, or 48 in).*
Width: *30 or 38 cm (12 or 15 in)*
Depth: *30 or 38 cm (12 or 15 in)*

Below: *The trim at the top of the tank should match the color of the stand and hood to help create a complete unit, rather than something that has been thrown together. Using black baseboard as a shelf at the bottom also helps to complete the picture.*

Right: Unassembled or ready-made cabinets are usually available in a choice of finishes. Some have cupboards below them in which you can safely and neatly conceal lighting units, external filters, and cables. You can also buy complete setups with integral, ready-wired hoods and filtration systems. Once you have plugged them in, simply add water, plants, and livestock.

Above: Tanks and cabinets such as this are designed as pieces of furniture and you can order a veneer to match your decor. The hood is part of the unit, as are sliding glass trays that form a condensation tray and give access to the tank. There is a shelf for the light to rest on and space at the rear of the hood for the lighting unit. Cutouts at the back allow for cables, air lines, and filter pipes.

Secondhand tanks

Local papers often carry advertisements for secondhand aquariums and if you know what you are doing, you might find a bargain. However, if you are a complete beginner, they can be a nightmare, as they often come complete with livestock that you have no idea how to care for. You also have no redress if the tank leaks or the equipment fails. Some aquatic dealers will offer secondhand tanks but these are often sold "as seen" and if they leak, too bad!

Sizes and capacities of standard tanks

Tank	Volume	Weight of water	
20x10x12 inches (50x25x30 cm)	10 gallons (37.8 L)	83 lbs	(38 kg)
24x12x12 inches (60x30x30 cm)	15 gallons (56.7 L)	125 lbs	(57 kg)
24x12x16 inches (60x30x40 cm)	20 gallons (75.7 L)	170 lbs	(76 kg)
30x12x12 inches (75x30x30 cm)	20 gallons (75.7 L)	170 lbs	(76 kg)
30x12x18 inches (75x30x45 cm)	29 gallons (109.7 L)	240 lbs	(109 kg)
36x12x16 inches (90x30x40 cm)	30 gallons (113.5 L)	250 lbs	(113 kg)

You may already have a place in mind for your aquarium, but you need to be sure that it is suitable. Fully set-up tanks are extremely heavy. When you consider that 1 liter of water weighs 1 kg (1 gallon weighs 8.3 lbs) and the 60 x 30 x 40 cm (24 x 12 x 16 in) tank we are featuring in this book holds approximately 76 liters (20 gallons), you can see that it will weigh 76 kg (166 lbs) without the weight of the tank itself, cabinet, rocks, gravel, etc. Your floor must be able to support this weight. If you have a concrete floor, this should pose no problems, but if you have floorboards, check which way the beams run and try to position the stand so that the legs are positioned over the beams rather than over the space between them. This is even more important for the larger-sized tanks. If you are placing the stand on a carpet, it is worth putting something under the legs of the stand to prevent it from cutting into the carpet.

The position of the tank in the room is, for the most part, a compromise, since it is rare to find the optimum conditions. Follow the directions given on the floor plan on page 11. Do consider the proximity of electrical outlets, since you will need one close to the aquarium. The last thing you want is to trip over wires trailing across the room! Safety considerations include not only making sure that electricity and water do not mix in the tank, but also placing the tank so that it is stable and will not fall onto anything or anyone, and no one can fall over it or the electricity supply to it.

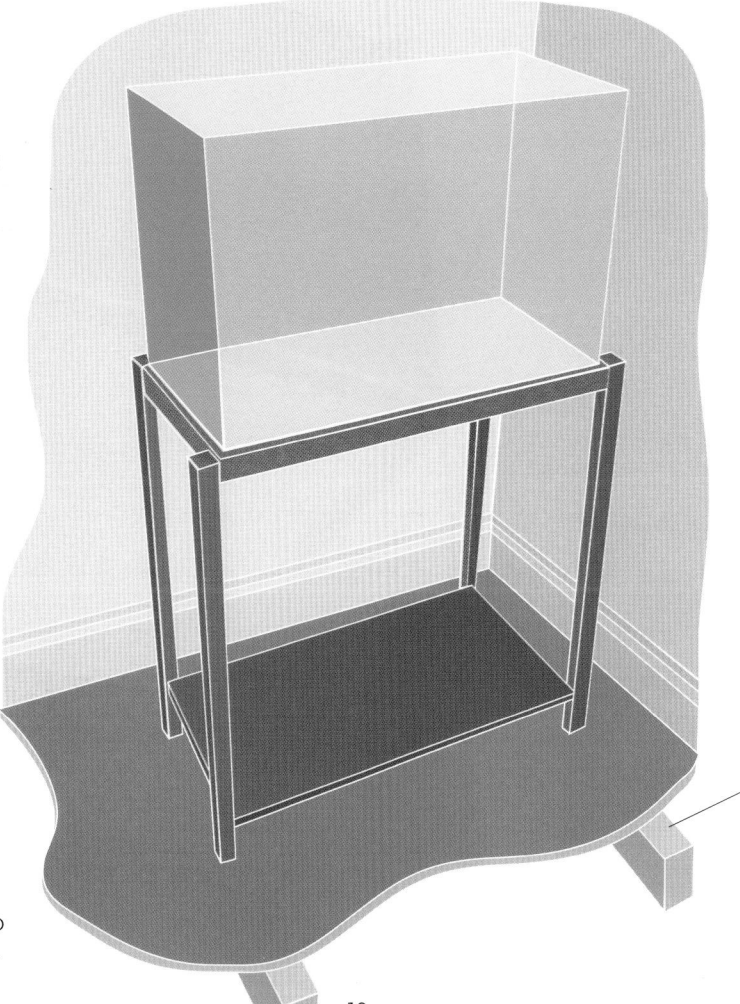

If you can, position the stand so that the weight of the finished unit is taken by the beams and not the floorboards.

Left: *Ideally, place the unit where it will not be affected by passing traffic through the room, light from windows, and heat from radiators. Pick a secluded corner where you can easily install and service the aquarium.*

Finding the best location for the aquarium

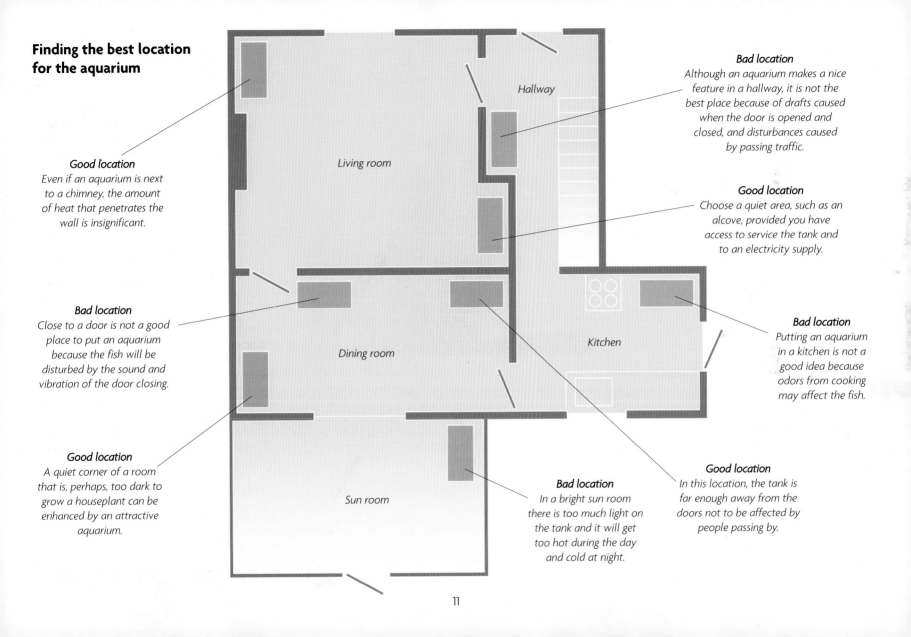

Good location
Even if an aquarium is next to a chimney, the amount of heat that penetrates the wall is insignificant.

Bad location
Although an aquarium makes a nice feature in a hallway, it is not the best place because of drafts caused when the door is opened and closed, and disturbances caused by passing traffic.

Good location
Choose a quiet area, such as an alcove, provided you have access to service the tank and to an electricity supply.

Bad location
Close to a door is not a good place to put an aquarium because the fish will be disturbed by the sound and vibration of the door closing.

Bad location
Putting an aquarium in a kitchen is not a good idea because odors from cooking may affect the fish.

Good location
A quiet corner of a room that is, perhaps, too dark to grow a houseplant can be enhanced by an attractive aquarium.

Bad location
In a bright sun room there is too much light on the tank and it will get too hot during the day and cold at night.

Good location
In this location, the tank is far enough away from the doors not to be affected by people passing by.

Hallway

Living room

Dining room

Kitchen

Sun room

To demonstrate setting up an aquarium we have chosen a standard-sized tank, 60 x 30 x 40 cm (24 x 12 x 16 in) high. If you are just starting out in fishkeeping, this size aquarium is ideal. It is compact enough for you to set up easily and will fit into a small house or apartment or, if you are a younger fishkeeper, in your bedroom if that is the only place available to you. Although relatively small, this size aquarium does hold enough water to prevent any rapid fluctuations in water conditions such as temperature and pH (degree of acidity or alkalinity). Any changes that do take place will happen gradually, thus preventing any great degree of stress on your fish. You will also have time to carry out whatever measures are necessary to alleviate the situation before it becomes a disaster, such as replace a heater that has failed.

Checklist

These are the items you will need for installation:

Tank and hood (may be an integral unit)	Scissors
	Craft knife
	Screwdrivers
	Pliers
Stand or cabinet	Cable clips or ties
Hammer	Adhesive tape
Baseboard for use on the stand	Insulation tape
	Water pitcher
Styrofoam tiles	Nail- or scrubbing brush
Level	A great deal of tea or coffee

Setting up the stand

It is advisable to have someone to help you assemble the stand and position the tank and stand; both are awkward and heavy. For safety, ensure that the area in which you are going to work is free of clutter – including children and pets – and remove any rugs or loose floor coverings that might trip you. Above all, allow yourself plenty of time to do the job. When you know what you are doing, it can take a couple of hours; if this is the first time you have set up an aquarium, allow twice this amount of time.

Above: *Stands may have feet that you can adjust by screwing them either up or down. Cabinets may require some packing under one edge to achieve the right level. In such a case, always make sure that what you use is safe.*

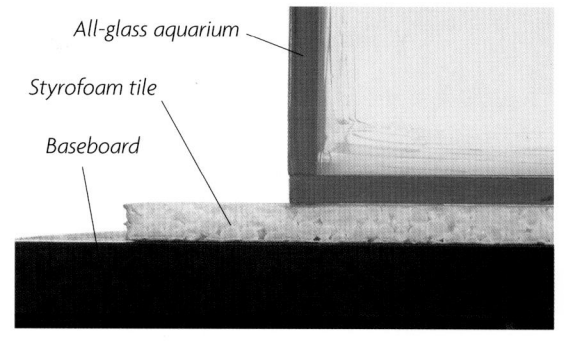

All-glass aquarium

Styrofoam tile

Baseboard

Above: *Always place glass tanks on a layer of styrofoam to even out imperfections in the baseboard. Even the smallest piece of grit can cause a fine crack in the base glass once the tank is full of water and gravel.*

When you bring your tank home, rest it on a flat surface while you set up the stand. Put styrofoam tiles on the floor and place the tank on top. Do not stand it partly on the floor and partly on a rug or other uneven floor covering, as the base may crack.

Following the manufacturer's instructions, put the stand together or assemble the cabinet (some are unassembled, some ready-constructed), and put it into position in the room. Check that it is level and adjust it as necessary. It is far safer and easier to do this now, before you put the tank on the stand.

Next, put a sturdy baseboard of melamine-coated chipboard on top of the stand (cut to size so that it fits comfortably), add a single layer of styrofoam tiles, accurately trimmed to the size of the tank base, and finally, place the tank carefully on top.

Cleaning and leveling the tank

Your next task is to clean the tank. It may look perfectly clean, but there is bound to be a fine film of dust inside it, which, if left where it is, will appear as a film on the water surface of the finished aquarium. Use a new cloth and water only to clean the tank, as any detergent can be lethal to livestock.

If you wish, you can conceal the white edge of the styrofoam with black insulation tape.

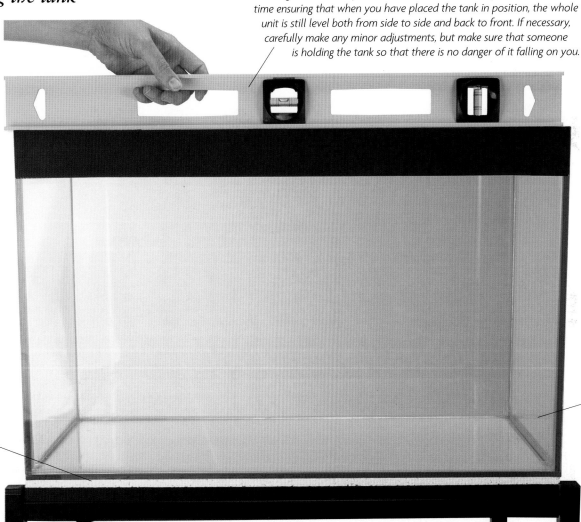

Having checked that your stand or cabinet is level, spend a little more time ensuring that when you have placed the tank in position, the whole unit is still level both from side to side and back to front. If necessary, carefully make any minor adjustments, but make sure that someone is holding the tank so that there is no danger of it falling on you.

It is worth filling the tank at this point to check for leaks – a very rare occurrence these days, but a problem that is easy to fix now. If it leaks, drain it and consult your dealer, who should replace it. If the tank is secondhand, drain it, dry it, and reseal it with silicone aquarium sealer.

Up to a point, the choice of substrate is a matter of taste, but you must also meet the needs of the fish you are going to keep and the type of filtration used.

Natural sand and gravel are available in various grades. The best types have rounded grains and are lime-free. (Gravels that originate from offshore sites may contain shell fragments and these can harden the water.) Some fish like to bury in the substrate and others feed by sifting through it. In this case, river sand or fine or medium gravels are suitable.

Another consideration is the type of filtration you are intending to use. Sand and fine gravel are too small for use with undergravel filters, as the grains fall into the slats in the filter plates and block them. Coarse gravel can be used with larger fish species but needs care because it is easy for debris and uneaten food to become trapped in the spaces between the grains.

Colored gravels are also available. Buy them only from a reliable aquatic outlet because in the past, dyes have been known to leach from some of the colored gravels, and these have proved fatal to fish.

River sand
Having rounded grains, river sand makes an excellent choice if you are keeping bottom-dwelling species. It is a noncompacting sand that allows the free passage of water and plant roots.

Coarse gravel
You can use coarse gravel in large setups or mix it with medium gravel to give a different look to an aquarium. It is especially useful for creating a streambed effect in the tank.

Colored gravels
Available as a mix such as this, or in individual colors, you need to be sure you can live with the gaudy effect it creates.

Fine gravel
This is a good choice for a smaller aquarium where medium or coarse gravel would look out of proportion.

Medium gravel
This is the standard gravel of the trade and it provides a suitable substrate for just about any size aquarium.

Black gravel
This can be used to dramatic effect to show off such boldly colored species as cardinal tetras.

Adding the gravel

Sand and gravel are dirty. Although washed before they leave the quarry, they are still dusty and must be washed thoroughly before use. Place small amounts in a bucket, add water, and agitate it using your hands or, perhaps, a wooden spoon kept for the purpose. Drain and repeat as necessary until the water runs clear.

Repeat until all your substrate is cleaned.

How much gravel?

If you are using an undergravel filter, the substrate needs to be about 6 cm (2.4 in) deep (see page 46). If you are not using an undergravel filter, it should be 4-5 cm (1.6-2 in) deep.

Carefully add the gravel to the aquarium, using your hands, a clean flowerpot, or a small bucket.

As you add the gravel you can spread it over the base. Some people like to keep the substrate flat; others like to bank it slightly so that it is lower at the front than the back. The choice is yours, but remember that it should be deep enough to put your plants in.

If you are using an undergravel filter, fit it to the base of the tank before you add the gravel.

There are two basic types of power filter: internal and external, which both work on the same principle of taking in water, passing it through the filter medium, and returning it to the aquarium. Movement of the water is generated by an electrical motor driving an impeller. The purpose of the filter medium is to provide a large area that beneficial bacteria can colonize. They break down much of the waste matter produced by the fish (see nitrogen cycle, page 26). Materials, such as activated carbon, can be incorporated to remove other toxic substances. The system we demonstrate uses an internal filter for ease of installation and operation and cost efficiency, but you could use an undergravel, canister, or external power filter instead.

Right: Internal power filters are suitable for the smaller aquarium. When servicing the tank, rinse the foam with tank water (removed when doing the water change). This way, you remove fine, clogging debris, but retain the beneficial bacteria.

Internal filter

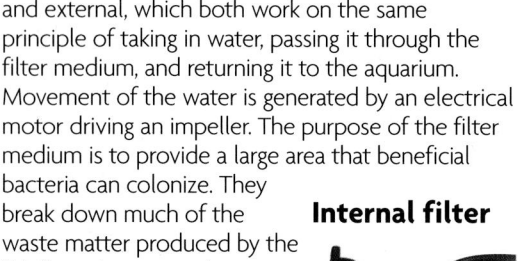

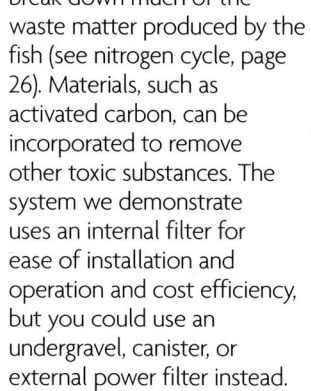

The foam cartridge houses the beneficial bacteria.

The plastic barrel has an internal divider to allow good water flow. This complete unit pushes onto the pump.

▶ Hints and tips

Check that the filter cable will reach the electrical source. Make sure you have easy access to the filter, as you will need to remove it completely from the carrier to service it. Stock up with spare suction cups and also a spare foam insert.

A submersible pump provides the power source. It may or may not have a venturi to aerate the water (see above).

The venturi effect

As water is pumped back into the tank, it can also be aerated by a venturi pipe. This accelerates the water flow and draws in a stream of air from above the surface.

Unpacking filters

Although internal power filters usually come with foam inserts, check that these are present. Remove any plastic packaging that may be around them or they will not work. Put the filter together as shown on this page.

Right: This internal power filter draws water in at the base of the unit and passes it through a block of filter foam. Models vary slightly, but the principle is the same.

Internal filter

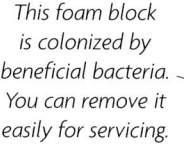

You can adjust the amount of air added to the returning water.

Water returns to the aquarium through this aperture.

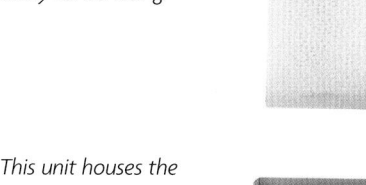

This foam block is colonized by beneficial bacteria. You can remove it easily for servicing.

This unit houses the submersible motor; attach it firmly to the aquarium glass.

Water is drawn in at the bottom of the unit. Make sure the passage of water is not restricted by any tank decorations.

Installing *an internal power filter*

Unpack your filter and read the manufacturer's instructions carefully, as different models vary slightly. Assemble the filter as instructed. Attach the suction cups supplied to the outside of the filter or carrying frame. You may need to wet them to get them to stick to the glass.

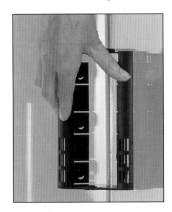

Carrying frames make removing the filter unit for cleaning and maintenance an easy procedure. Attach the carrier to the rear corner of the aquarium, pressing it firmly against the glass. Be careful when inserting the filter into the carrier. Do not force it or you may break the carrier.

Position the filter with the nozzle facing outward. Direct the outflow across the diagonal of the aquarium.

Check with the manufacturer's instructions and position the filter head at or just below the water surface.

Allow a space between the base of the filter and the substrate to avoid the accumulation of dirt and debris and to allow free passage of water into and around the filter canister.

Tropical fish and plants require warmth to keep them alive. Outside their preferred range, their bodies cease to function properly and they die. The temperature of the water also affects its oxygen-holding capacity; the warmer the water, the less oxygen it can hold, and species that are not accustomed to lower oxygen levels will be seen gasping at the surface. In cooler conditions, the fish tend to slow down and rest near the bottom. Plants may put on a spurt of growth and become straggly or they may disintegrate. Fortunately, with modern technology, maintaining the water at a natural level of 23-24°C (73-75°F) is quite easy to accomplish using one of the heating units available from your local aquarium dealer. Now, you may be thinking that in a centrally heated home you do not need a heater – not so! During the day, the ambient room temperature may keep the aquarium water just warm enough. However, it will not raise the water temperature to that of the room; the water will be several degrees lower than the room temperature, so what happens during the night when the heating is turned down to allow you to sleep in comfort? The tank temperature drops, perhaps to critical or even fatal levels. It is therefore up to you to provide the correct temperature range and a heater-thermostat will accomplish this.

Power outages

There may come a time when you have a power outage. Short outages are not a problem, as the tank will cool slowly and then warm slowly, causing the fish no great stress provided it does not cool too far. It is worth calling your utility company to get an idea of how long the lack of service will last. If it is protracted, wrap a blanket around and over the tank to slow down chilling. If you have an alternative source of heating, fill plastic bottles with hot water and float them in the aquarium. In most cases, the reduction in the water temperature is not the main cause for concern.

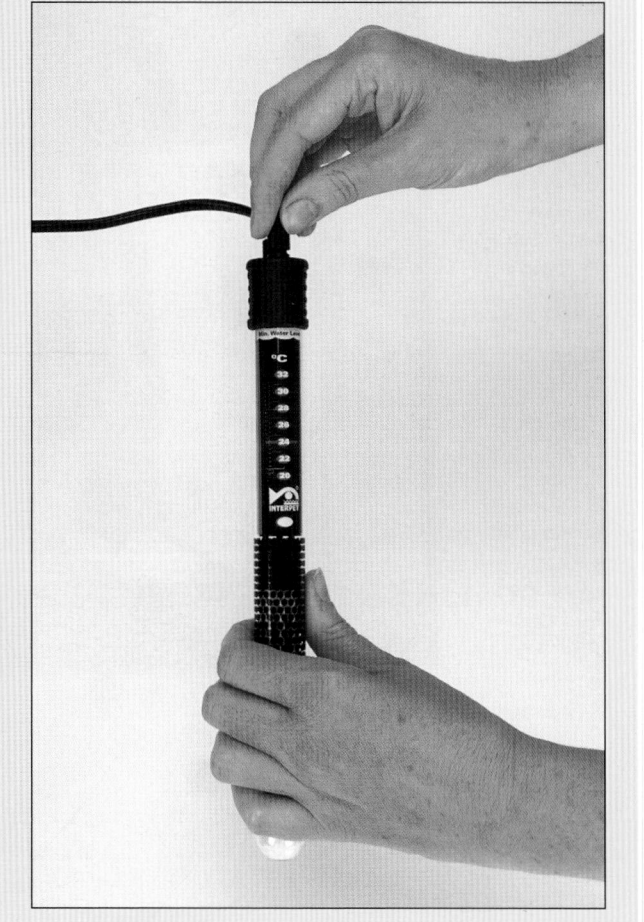

Types of heaters

The combined submersible heater-thermostat is the ideal choice for the novice fishkeeper. It is easy to regulate and, being submersible, cannot be easily tampered with once set at the desired temperature. Separate heaters are also available in the form of submersible heaters or undertank heating mats. Both are controlled by either external or internal thermostats. (Children love fiddling with the knobs on an external thermostat, so be careful where you place them!) There are also power filters on the market that incorporate a heating unit in the system.

Right: *Combined heater-thermostats are easy to adjust by turning the knob at the top until you reach the desired temperature. Models are available calibrated in °C or °F or both scales side by side. Some units have a light to indicate whether it is on or off. Make sure you can see this.*

Installing the heater

Unpack the heater-thermostat and keep the instructions that tell you how to position and adjust it. Read these carefully, as there may be variations between manufacturers. Attach the suction cups. Check to see what temperature it is set at and adjust if necessary.

Right: *The suction cups are usually supplied detached from the unit. Place them over the heater and slide them along so that one is near the top and the other near the bottom. You may need to wet them to stick them to the glass. Always keep spare suction cups and a spare heater-thermostat in stock.*

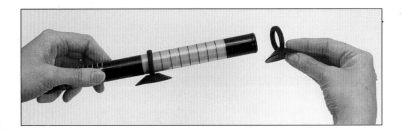

Most manufacturers recommend placing the heater at an angle (heating element at the bottom), so that as the heat rises, it does not go straight past the thermostat.

Leave a small space between the bottom of the heater and the substrate. Do not cover units with substrate as they will overheat. Make sure the water flow is not obstructed by any tank decorations placed in front of the heater.

As the water is circulated by the filter, it will pass the heater and warm up.

What size heater?
The size heater you need (wattage) will depend on the size of your aquarium. As a guide, you need 50 watts per 27 liters (6 gallons) of water.

Safety first
Never turn on the heater until the tank is full of water.

STAGE 7 Choosing and preparing wood

For details of synthetic wood see pages 48-49

Wood can be very useful in the aquarium, being not only physically pleasing to look at, but also forming an important part in the diet of some fish. It has a much softer look than rocks, both in shape and texture. Bogwood and mopani, shown here, should be available from your local aquatic outlet. Vine roots may also be available. Do not be tempted to collect wood from the wild, as you can never be sure what you are collecting; beetles like to use dead wood and the thought of beetles and their grubs appearing in your tank is not a pleasant one!

Wood is dusty and dirty, but it will have been washed before you buy it. However, you should check it over and remove any dead bits of moss or fine roots that may be sticking to it. Most of this can be done with a dry brush but you may need to wash and scrub it. You may need to soak larger pieces of wood in a bucket (or, if they are very large, the bathtub) to release some of the tannins that will stain the water. Change the water every day or so until the staining is at an acceptable level (carbon in the filter will help reduce some of this in the aquarium).

It is often thought that varnishing wood will prevent tannins from leaching into the water. However, wood is a natural substance with many crevices that are impossible to penetrate with varnish. Water does manage to get into these crevices and can lift the varnish, rendering it useless. The other problem arises with fish that eat wood as part of their diet or chew on it to create breeding hollows, such as bristlenose catfish (*Ancistrus* sp.). Varnish would kill them. Washing and/or soaking wood is by far the best option.

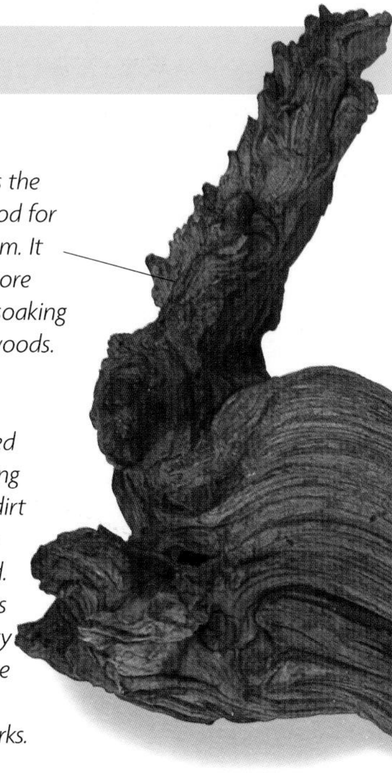

Bogwood is the standard wood for the aquarium. It requires more cleaning and soaking than other woods.

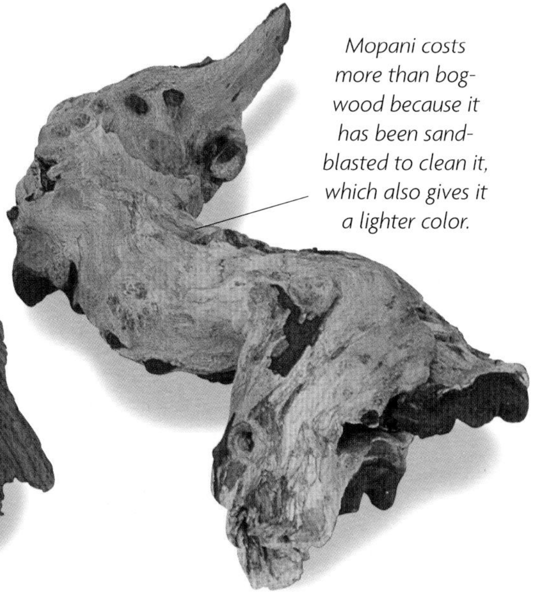

Mopani costs more than bog-wood because it has been sand-blasted to clean it, which also gives it a lighter color.

Below: *A stiff-bristled nailbrush or scrubbing brush will dislodge dirt and debris from the crevices in the wood. Brush off as much as possible from the dry wood. You may have to wet the wood to remove stubborn marks.*

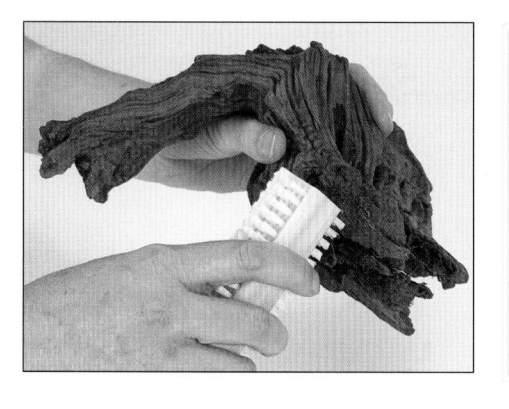

Using cork

Cork can be used in the aquarium. Some pieces look as though they have just been peeled off the tree and need a good soaking to waterlog them. Dry them out and attach them to a piece of slate using silicone sealer. Bury the slate in the gravel to prevent the cork from floating away.

Adding the wood

Put the wood in place and embed it into the substrate to ensure that it does not fall over. Position it so that it will not disrupt access to equipment that may need to be replaced or serviced. If you find that the wood will not quite fit your tank, try to break it carefully, rather than cutting it with a saw. Look at the wood and be guided by its shape and graining; if it looks like a tree root coming down into the tank, use it as such. If it is more like a fallen branch, it may be best to lay it down in the tank. At this stage, with no water in the tank, you can play around with it easily.

Natural wood

The size and shape of the wood you choose is up to you. Try it out against a tank of similar proportions to yours to gain an idea of how it will look in your aquarium. Make sure you buy a natural piece that does not have any sawed edges, as these look very unnatural when you see them in the tank and are very difficult to conceal with plants.

You can place wood in front of the heater, but make sure it does not rest against it. Take care not to knock and break the heater when putting it in place. The wood is not only part of the aquarium decor, it also serves a practical function by concealing the heater.

Do not place any wood in front of the filter or you will obstruct the water flow. It is worth checking that your piece of wood sinks before you put it in the tank; some have been known to float!

For details of synthetic rocks see pages 48-49

It would seem to be a simple task to find rocks for your aquarium; just go and pick some up. Not so! Unless you know what you are doing, "just picking up rocks" can be a disaster. If you happen to pick the wrong ones, rocks can change the water chemistry in your aquarium to the detriment of your fish. Your local aquatic outlet will provide a selection of rocks for both fresh and marine aquariums, so be sure to check with them that you have chosen the right ones. Bear in mind that waterworn rocks look much more natural than broken, angular pieces, and try to stick to one type of rock rather than mixing different colors and textures. If you want to build up a rocky structure in the aquarium, glue together cleaned, dry rocks with silicone sealant before putting them in the tank. This will prevent rock structures from falling down.

Below: *Most of the rocks shown here are suitable for a general community aquarium. They are inert, which means they will not leach anything harmful into the water, and hard enough to provide spawning sites for fish should they wish to use them.*

Right: *Rocks need washing; indeed, they need scrubbing. The amount of dirt that can stick to a seemingly clean rock is amazing, especially if it has deep crevices, such as this piece of weathered rock. Be sure to remove all dust, dirt, and pieces of moss or lichens to prevent them from fouling your tank.*

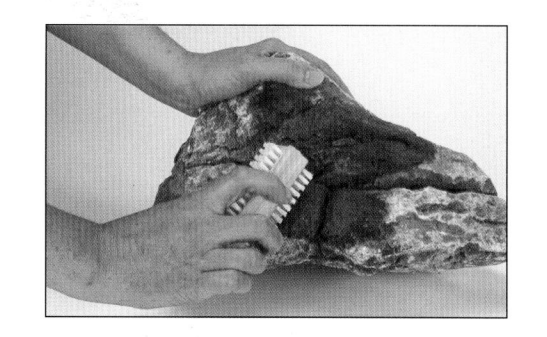

Unsuitable rocks

Avoid rocks that will change your water chemistry. Tufa is used in marine tanks and both tufa and limestone are also used in hardwater freshwater setups to help maintain water hardness. These are not suited to a tropical freshwater tank such as the one we are setting up.

Rocks in shades of green and gray increase the range of color available.

Weathered limestone has natural fissures that create interesting textures in the aquarium, but should only be used in tanks whose inhabitants need harder water (such as rift lake cichlids).

The dark tones of slate provide dramatic contrast.

Warm colors glow in the tank lights.

The grainy texture and solidity of granite add "weight" to tank displays.

Placing the rocks

1 Carefully plan where you are going to place your rocks. They are heavy and you may need help to lift and place large pieces. Wriggle them down into the substrate until they are resting on the base glass to prevent fish from undermining them.

2 When you are satisfied with the position of the main piece(s), you can add the smaller ones until you have completed your layout. Remember to leave enough room to replace or service any equipment in the aquarium and avoid disrupting the water flow from the filter.

Above: Smaller waterworn pebbles can help to take the edge off larger angular rocks.

If you were to accidentially drop a rock from a sufficient height, you could crack the tank. Make sure you have a good grip on it as you place it in the tank.

Be careful when adding heavy rocks that you do not accidentally damage the equipment you have just installed.

Creating stable rock features

If you are creating a cavelike structure with rocks piled on top of each other, it is essential that you place the base rocks safely. Fish are more powerful than you might think and it is not unheard-of for parts of a supposedly safe structure to move, fall, and crack the aquarium glass. Remember: structures must be stable.

Before you start to keep any fish, it is best to discover what type of water you have and keep fish that are happy in it. This is easier and more reliable than trying to change the water chemistry. Water companies take the raw water from whatever source and treat it to provide safe drinking water for our homes. That water source could be anything from a hill stream to a subterranean aquifer, and the water could be soft and acidic, hard and alkaline, high in oxygen, low in oxygen, warm, cool, or any variation.

Just as we need clean, fresh air to breathe, fish require clean, fresh water to live in. If the air in our area becomes polluted, we can move to another area. However, if their water becomes unfit, fish cannot move to another water source. And in an aquarium, it is not just a matter of pollution control, but also a question of the water chemistry. For example, fish that live in acidic conditions cannot tolerate alkaline ones. Each fish species needs water suited to its requirements if it is to survive.

Above: In the lower courses of rivers, water levels drop over the summer, the movement is sluggish, and the oxygen content may be low. Such waters can also be high in phosphates and nitrates brought in by the runoff from surrounding agricultural land.

Tap water

We all take water for granted. It flows from our taps, is clean and clear, and ready for us to drink, but does that make it right for our fish? The water provided by your local water company is treated to render it fit for human consumption.

Chlorine gas is commonly used for purification and if it has been heavily used, you will smell it when you draw water from your tap. If you allow the water to stand for 24 hours, the chlorine will disperse. You can speed up the process by using an airstone to agitate the water.

Another chemical added by water companies is chloramine. This is more difficult to deal with, as it does not disperse naturally. If this is used in your area, you will need to buy a water conditioner to neutralize it. (This will also deal with the chlorine.) Check with your water company to see what is added to your water. If you get on friendly terms with them, they will also let you know if they are intending to flush the water mains with anything to kill bugs that may affect fish.

Other pollutants of tap water include nitrates and phosphates that leach into the water from agricultural fertilizers. Levels can vary over the course of the year.

Water hardness

This is a measure of the dissolved mineral salts in the water – the more salts, the harder it is. As water passes through rocks and soil, some of the minerals contained in them dissolve into the water. This means that water originating from limestone aquifers is hard, while water from other areas may be softer. For aquarium purposes, hardness is the amount of calcium carbonate ($CaCO_3$) measured in degrees of hardness (°dH) or parts per million (ppm). Buy a test kit, check your water hardness, and choose your fish to suit. You might come across the terms "temporary hardness" and "permanent hardness." Temporary hardness can be removed by boiling the water, but permanent hardness cannot.

Filling the tank

The easiest way to fill your tank is with a pitcher. At this stage you can use cold or warm water, as no livestock or plants are present. Gently pour the water over a flat stone to avoid disturbing the substrate too much. It takes time but is better than destroying your aquarium decor. If you have no suitable stones in your setup, pour the water into a saucer.

Use a clean pitcher to start filling the tank. As the water level rises, you can add the water by slowly pouring from a bucket, checking that it is not disturbing the substrate too much.

Tank hygiene

If you use a bucket, make sure that it is free of any residues of cleaning products. It is much better to keep a bucket solely for aquarium use.

The pH scale

The pH scale is used to determine the acidity or alkalinity of the water. It runs from 0 (extremely acidic) to 14 (extremely alkaline), with 7 being termed neutral. It is a logarithmic scale, each step being 10 times the previous one. This is why seemingly small changes can have dramatic effects. Test kits and electronic meters are available to measure pH.

The more you clean the gravel before you put it in the aquarium, the less likely it is to cause cloudiness as you add the water. Once the aquarium is full, carefully rearrange any substrate you have disturbed by too-vigorous pouring.

At this stage, you will be tempted to put in your plants, but wait at least 24 hours. This will allow you to check that the heater and filter are functioning properly; if there is a problem, it is easier to fix it now. At best you may need to replace or adjust the heater; at worst, the tank might leak. All these problems are easier to solve without plants in the tank. You will also give the water time to settle at the correct temperature. Plants, like fish, are tropical and will become chilled if they are plunged into water that is too cold. After a couple of hours, check the water temperature with your thermometer. Just dip it into the water to take a reading. There is no point in putting it in its final position as it will only be in the way when you begin to add the plants.

Thinking about the fish to add

Another decision to make at this point is which fish to keep. The number of fish you can keep in one tank depends on the surface area of the water. For tropical freshwater species you need 75 sq cm (12 sq in) of surface area per 2.5 cm (1 in) of fish body length, not including the tail. This tank will hold a total of 60 cm/24 in (body length) of fish. You could start with four cherry barbs or White Cloud Mountain minnows, or a pair of platies. The total length of each of these groups of fish is about a quarter of the total allowable for this tank. Use this as a guide when adding more fish later. If you add a quarter of your fish every 10 days, you will have a fully stocked tank just as the filtration system has matured.

How the nitrogen cycle works

While we are waiting for the system to be ready for us to add the first plants, we should explore some natural chemical processes that take place within an aquarium. The most important of these is the circulation of nitrogen-containing compounds, commonly known as the nitrogen cycle. This natural process is the means by which dead and decaying waste products containing nitrogen are converted by bacteria from poisonous compounds, such as ammonia, into harmless substances, such as nitrates. These are then taken up by the plants. It will start happening in your tank as soon as you set it up and the filtration system will help it along. As the filtration system becomes colonized by helpful bacteria, it becomes more efficient. However, as soon as you add fish, there is a system overload and it takes a few days for the numbers of bacteria to build up to cope with the extra waste. This is why it is best to add a few fish at a time, not all of them at once. The first thing to happen is that bacteria break down the toxic ammonia excreted by fish and produced by decomposition. This is converted to less harmful, although still dangerous, nitrites, which are converted to much less harmful nitrates. In an ideal world, all the nitrates would be taken up by the plants, but in an aquarium, it is not that simple.

We usually overload our tanks with fish that produce too much waste for the plants to use. The result is high nitrate levels. The only way to remove these is by carrying out regular partial water changes.

Ammonia is excreted by fish through the gills and in their waste products.

Nitrates are taken up by the plants as a fertilizer.

Ammonia is converted to nitrites by bacteria in the filtration system.

Nitrites are converted to nitrates by bacteria in the filtration system.

Switching on the system

The water level in the tank can be 2.5 cm (1 in) or so below the final level but should cover the heater and filter to at least the recommended levels. You are then ready to switch on the system. For the time being, you can rest the condensation tray over the tank to prevent dust and debris from entering, and to deter any cats or children from tampering with it.

Make sure the heater-thermostat is submerged.

Any cloudiness in the water should be removed by the filtration system.

Safety first

Make sure that all the equipment is properly installed (submersed to the correct levels and firmly attached) before switching on the power supply.

Check that the filter system is working and adjust the direction and rate of flow if necessary.

Plants play a vital role in a well-balanced aquarium, because they help to lower nitrate levels (see page 26). Choose aquatic plants, rather than the houseplants that are sometimes sold for aquariums.

Select plants by size, leaf shape, and color. Use tall ones for the back of the aquarium, medium and short ones for the center and front. Plants are sold either potted or bare-rooted. Both are fine, provided the plants look healthy (see page 33).

Put in each plant individually; it seems time-consuming but is well worthwhile. (After all, you would not plant cabbages or roses three or four to a hole and expect them all to grow into healthy plants.) Allow enough space between the plants for the light to reach the substrate. Plant in rows and stagger the rows so that the whole grouping looks like a wall of plants from the front.

This healthy Bacopa *is growing in a planting medium contained in a small plastic basket.*

Above: *It is worth unpotting a plant like this* Bacopa. *As you can see, it yields several cuttings that you can plant separately. If left in the pot, the lower leaves would turn yellow because the light could not reach them, and eventually you would see ugly bare stems. At worst, rot could set in.*

It is especially important that Cryptocoryne *does not have badly damaged leaves, as these quickly rot back to the crown.*

Left: *Unraveled from its potting medium, this* Cryptocoryne *reveals that it is made up of several small plants. Giving each plant its own space to grow creates a carpet of plants in the aquarium.*

Vallisneria

Vallisneria *creates height at the back of the aquarium. The straplike leaves are quite tough and will not be damaged by the gentle flow from the filter. If any plants are dislodged, just push them back in again. Before planting, check each plant and remove any brown leaves. If left on, these could rot, which could spread to the crown of the plant and kill it. Vallis plants are slim and there is a great temptation to plant them as a clump; resist it!*

Planting Vallisneria

Gently hold the plant near the base and, using a finger of the same hand, make a hole in the gravel. This prevents the stem and roots from bruising as you slide the plant into the substrate, just deep enough to keep it from coming loose. This takes a little practice, but persevere.

Start by planting a row at the back of the aquarium and work forward. Planting depth is dictated by the type of plant. In this case, look at the white area at the base of the plant; the top of the white area should be at the surface.

Safety first

Switch off all electrical equipment before starting work on the aquarium. As an extra precaution, also unplug it from the socket

Plant the next plant about 2cm (0.8in) away from the first. Continue like this until you have a row of the required length along the back of the tank.

Repeat the process for the next row about 2cm (0.8in) in front of the first, placing the plants in front of the spaces in the row behind. Repeat as necessary to make more rows or partial rows.

Before you start planting, it is worth dropping the water level slightly. This not only stops you from splashing water all over the place, it also saves you from getting your sleeves wet!

For details of other suitable plants see pages 50-55

Some plants are sold as cuttings. They are sold loose, in bunches, or potted. Whichever is available to you, apply the same rules. Look for healthy plants with good green leaves and no dead or dying leaves or stems. Cuttings are particularly prone to rotting at the base because the stems are damaged when they are thrust into the gravel. This is even more likely when they are gathered in a clump and held together with a metal strip, which bruises the stems, creating a site of infection.

These plants have a great advantage in the aquarium—you can cut them to the required length to create your desired design. They naturally grow quite tall and may be used toward the rear of the aquarium, but they can also be cut to shorter lengths so that each row is slightly shorter than the one behind, thus creating a wall of plants.

Left: *Carefully remove the metal strip from the base of the* Cabombas *and gently separate each cutting. Take your time.* Cabomba *is a delicate plant that bruises easily.*

Left: *Using a pair of sharp scissors, cut away the bare, damaged stem just below a leaf joint and discard the damaged portion. If you need shorter plants you can cut further up the stem.*

The plants used in this aquarium

Vallisneria spiralis *(about 25 rooted pieces)*
Cabomba *sp. (about 30 individual cuttings)*
Ludwigia *sp. (about 10 individual cuttings)*
Bacopa *sp. (about 5 individual cuttings)*
Amazon swordplant *(1 complete plant with roots)*
Cryptocoryne *sp. (about 6 rooted small plants)*

Although the number of plants shown here seems rather high, remember that many plants are sold as bundles of cuttings that you can plant separately.

Aquarium plants sold as cuttings

The main plants available as cuttings are Bacopa, Cabomba, Hygrophila, Ludwigia, and water wisteria. Treat all these, and any other cuttings you come across, as described here.

Planting Cabomba

Start planting at the rear of the tank and work toward the front, taking care not to pull out the plants that are already in place. As this tank is planted, we are leaving an open space in the foreground so that bottom-dwelling fish can come out and feed.

> ## Hints and tips

When you get your plants home, unpack them carefully. Once prepared for planting, lay them out on a tray in shallow, warm water to prevent them from drying out. If necessary, cover them with a plastic bag.

Allow yourself plenty of time to plant the aquarium. Rushing the process can damage the plants.

If you cannot find all the plants you want in one trip, do not panic; you can always add one or two later on.

Put in each plant individually. Space the plants so that their leaves just touch (it will vary from species to species) and light can reach the substrate.

Choose plants with colors and leaf shapes that complement each other. The coarse leaves of the Vallisneria *are ideal for concealing a filter, whereas the softer-leaved* Cabomba *would be damaged in this position. It is far better used in a quieter area to soften the edges of the wood.*

Continue planting until you have created a wall of plants across the back of the aquarium, but avoid placing the Cabomba in the direct flow from the filter.

Planting the aquarium

For details of other suitable plants see pages 50-55

You can use large plants, such as Amazon sword-plants, to provide a focal point in the aquarium. Since they grow quite big, a single plant in a tank of this size is sufficient. However, the pygmy chain swordplant, *Echinodorus tennellus,* remains small and is suitable for the front of the tank, where it will carpet the substrate.

You can also use *Cryptocoryne* as a spot plant, with several of the taller species planted close by and low-growing varieties as carpet plants in the mid to foreground area. Once established, these spread by runners and you will need to keep them in check, or they will overrun the tank. These plants are available bare-rooted or potted; you may find up to six or seven *Cryptocoryne* plantlets per pot.

2 Gently pry away the growing medium. This is usually wrapped around the base of the plant. When you unwrap it, you should reveal the base of the plant and the root system. The healthy roots are the white ones.

3 Carefully remove any small pieces of growing medium attached to the roots. If the medium looks like damp paper, it will come away easily. If it resembles a blanket of coarse filter wool, it is more difficult to remove.

Preparing Amazon swordplants

1 Carefully remove the basket from the growing medium. There may be some roots protruding through the basket; be careful not to break too many of these.

Basket or no basket?

You can put the plants into the tank in their basket, but even if you hide the basket with gravel, the fish soon excavate it, and it then looks unsightly. The other problem is that several plants are often put into one pot to make it look like a large plant and these will not grow to their full potential in the overcrowded conditions of the basket.

4 Separate the plants and remove any dead or damaged roots and leaves. Now they are ready to plant.

Planting Amazon swordplants

Hold the prepared plant near the base and gently push it into the substrate, using your fingers to create the hole as you push into the gravel. Make sure that the roots are buried in the substrate, or the plant will float free.

Place the plant where it will be seen to full advantage and will also have room to spread its leaves. We have chosen to place it in front of the wood but behind the pebbles.

Amazon swordplants have quite a large spread of leaves, which create shaded areas. These are ideal places for low-growing shade-loving species, such as some of the small Cryptocoryne.

Choosing plants

Always look for healthy green leaves (or red if this is the natural color of the plant) with no signs of yellowing. Choose plants with a short distance between whorls of leaves (a lengthy space is a sign of forced growth). Avoid plants with damaged leaves (holes or tears) or falling leaves, plants with damaged crowns, and plants with damaged stems.

Continue to plant the tank. You can conceal the edges of this rock with a thicket of Ludwigia to the side and perhaps one or two small Cryptocoryne between it and the pebbles. When you have finished planting, put the top back on the tank.

33

The hood houses the light source that promotes healthy plant growth and allows you to see your fish. There are different styles of hoods, so you may need to modify this sequence for your hood. You can buy fully fitted hoods that include the lighting system and an integral condensation cover. These comply with local safety regulations and are easy to install. Place them on the tank and connect to the power supply. Other tanks have integral hoods and the strip light sits on a glass shelf. Make sure you know how to prepare your hood. Unpack it and the starter unit and check that you have everything you need.

Lighting tubes

Fluorescent tubes are now the industry standard. They have been developed in several colors to imitate daylight, promote plant growth, and enhance fish color. They can also be used in combination; for example, a white light (bottom) plus a pink light (top) covers the full spectrum and enhances the fish color. Blue is normally for marines and invertebrates. For a beginner, a good white light is the most suitable.

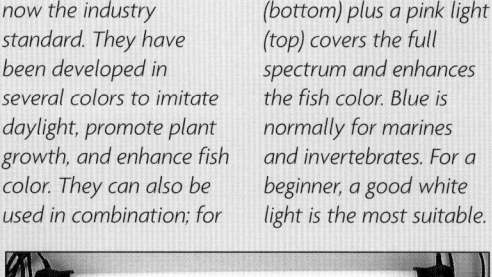

Fitting a fluorescent tube in the hood

1 Fit the clips with their nuts and bolts into the hood. If the holes for this are not predrilled, you will need to drill some. Tighten the nuts by hand and check that the clips are in the right way to hold the tube.

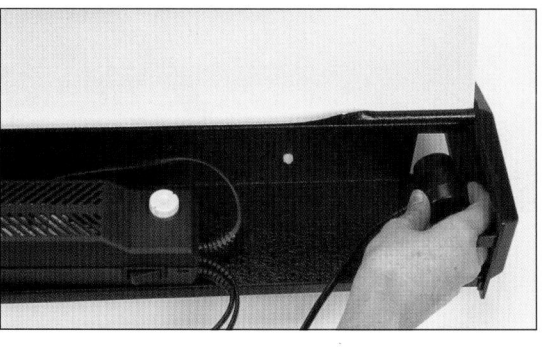

3 Feed the flying wires through the holes at either side of the rear chamber. The end caps that fit onto each end of the fluorescent tube have a plastic collar to create a watertight connection – essential in the aquarium.

2 Place the starter unit into the back chamber of the hood. This unit is quite heavy, so work on a table or on the floor so that nothing accidentally falls into the tank and breaks either the tank or the equipment in it.

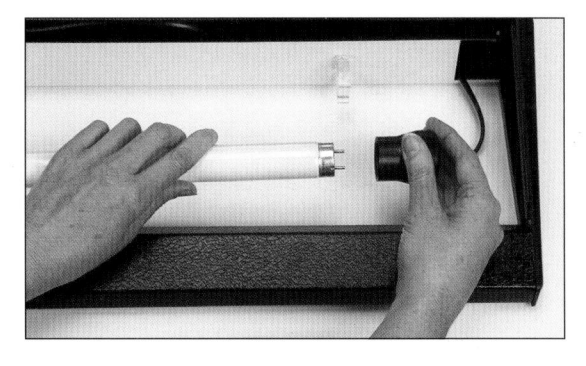

4 Connect the tube carefully, making sure that the pins on the tube fit into the holes in the end caps. Do not cut away the black covering of the end caps to make things easier; it is there for your safety to keep water and electricity apart.

Installing the lighting in the hood

Align the tube with the front of the clips and gently push it into position. Be careful not to use so much force that you break the clips or the tube. You may need help when installing the light, as the front flap of the hood can easily fall forward onto your hands and it is useful if someone else holds it open. It is lightweight and does not hurt, but it is annoying when it happens.

The inside of the hood is white, which helps to reflect light back into the aquarium.

Cable ties are useful to keep straggling wires neat in the rear chamber.

Gently pull any excess length of flying wire back through the holes in the hood and lay them neatly in the rear chamber.

Hints and tips

Before installation, connect the tube to the flying wires and plug in the unit to check that everything is working. Then switch off, unplug from the electrical outlet, and dismantle before installing in the hood.

The condensation tray serves three purposes: It limits water loss by reducing evaporation, it prevents the small amount of evaporation from reaching the electrical fittings of the lighting unit, and it stops fish from jumping out of the tank. Condensation trays can be made of plastic, as here, or glass. You may need to modify the tray to accommodate the cables and pipes, unless your system has an integral condensation cover.

Some aquariums are supplied complete with glass condensation trays that slide on runners to allow easy access to the tank. Because they are made of a clear material, they allow the free passage of light into the aquarium. If this is reduced, plant growth can suffer. Make sure that the cover glass is kept clean at all times. Regularly wipe it with a damp cloth to keep it free of algae, and to remove a buildup of salts and any remnants of flake food that have spilled when feeding your fish.

2 Check that wires and/or pipes can pass easily through the cut-off section. Do not forget that with this type of condensation tray you will also need to cut out a corner at the front of the tank to allow you to feed the fish.

3 Finally, put the modified condensation tray in place over the aquarium.

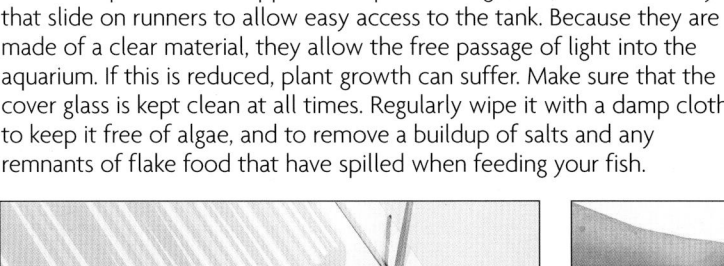

1 Lightweight plastic covers are easy to cut with sharp scissors. If necessary, trim the sides as well as the corners. Make a single diagonal cut rather than a rectangular shape, as the plastic tends to split from the corners of such a hole.

Fitting the hood

Whether you are using an integral hood complete with lights or you have fitted one out yourself, be careful when placing it on the aquarium. This can be a tricky operation because the hood, complete with its light fitting, is quite heavy. If you are unsure about lifting it and placing it on the tank by yourself, ask someone to help you. It is much safer than dropping the hood into the tank! As the unit's wire is trailing out of the back of the hood, either put the plug in your pocket so that you do not trip over it, or coil the wire and put it out of the way in the rear chamber of the hood.

Be careful

As you fit the hood onto the tank, remember that the condensation tray is in place. If the hood with its heavy lighting unit slips, it can crash straight through the tray. Be careful!

Make sure that the hood is the right way around when you put it on the tank. The chamber housing the starter unit goes at the back of the aquarium.

Just before you put on the hood, stand back and look at the aquarium and make any minor adjustments to the placement of the plants and decorations.

Backgrounds are a matter of personal taste. The best ones are plastic and available on a roll, so they are both waterproof and easy to cut to size. If you have chosen a picture background and you need to trim it to fit the height of your tank, the design will dictate whether you trim the top or the bottom. For example, if it shows a planted aquarium, trim the bottom, or you will see the cut-off tops of plants through the tank. However, if you have chosen the tree roots, the top would be the best place to cut. Choose a background that complements your tank; a solid wall of rock behind plants would look out of place. We have chosen a neutral background – black – as this adds depth to the aquarium and brings out the colors in the plants and fish.

Sunken cities complement similar ornaments used as tank decor.

Rockwork adds depth to a tank predominantly decorated with rocks of a similar color and texture.

Plant scenes blend in well with planted tanks.

Trees and logs make a useful background for a larger aquarium.

Adding the thermometer

Place the thermometer where it is easy to read and accessible. Avoid putting it in the direct flow from the filter or it will get thrown against the glass. This internal thermometer is more versatile than the stick-on form as you can remove it to check the temperature when doing water changes. Place a stick-on thermometer where it will not be affected by sunlight falling on the tank or the heat from nearby radiators.

Right: A good place for the thermometer is in a front corner so that the top is just below the water surface.

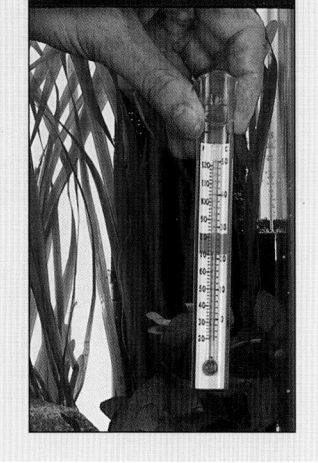

Left: Attach the background to the back of the tank on the outside. Secure it with clear adhesive tape along the entire length of each side. This is sufficient for a tank of this size, but on wider tanks you may need more tape along the top and bottom as well. You may need someone to help you with this stage.

This roll has a black background on one side and blue on the other. The blue grades from light to dark across its width. Both provide a neutral background.

Maturing the tank

The tank is now complete – except for the fish. Switch on all the equipment and check that it is working. Now you need a little time and patience – the two things you cannot buy. Fish tanks are not instant; they need time to mature. Total maturation of the filtration system takes about 36 days. Ideally, you should wait that long before adding any fish, but you could add the first few fish after 7-10 days, and a few more a week or so later. This way you build up your full complement of fish over a five- to six-week period or even longer. Do not try to cheat the system. A little time and patience at this stage will result in a well-balanced, healthy aquarium for your fish to enjoy.

The lighting should be running for about 12 hours a day to promote healthy plant growth. Remember to keep the condensation tray clean so that maximum light reaches the plants.

During the next few weeks, aerobic bacteria will be colonizing the filter sponge. These will help to break down the waste products from the fish.

Check the thermometer twice a day and keep a note of the reading. Expect it to fluctuate by a degree or so from day to night and even day to day, especially in hot weather. A log (diary) will help you to build up a natural pattern and, should this change, to spot a potential problem.

Plants will start to grow, taking nourishment from the water. If nothing seems to be happening, do not be too quick to remove them. They will first put out roots to anchor themselves before putting out new leaves.

Introducing the first fish is one of the most exciting aspects of a new tank. Choose your fish with care, because they will be with you for a few years. The aquarium dealer will pack your fish in a plastic bag containing a small amount of water and a great deal of air. This should then be put into a paper bag, as fish kept in the dark during transportation suffer less stress. This in turn is often placed into a carrier bag. If the weather is very hot or cold, it is a wise precaution to take along an insulated box or bag to ensure that the fish do not overheat or chill on the trip home. Go straight home after buying your fish so that they spend the least possible time in transit and are therefore subject to less stress.

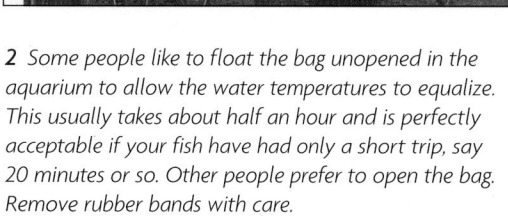

1 When you arrive home, carefully remove the outer carrier bag and the inner paper bag.

2 Some people like to float the bag unopened in the aquarium to allow the water temperatures to equalize. This usually takes about half an hour and is perfectly acceptable if your fish have had only a short trip, say 20 minutes or so. Other people prefer to open the bag. Remove rubber bands with care.

3 If the fish have had a longer trip home, it is always worth opening the bag to provide some fresh air for them. Carefully roll down the sides of the bag and hook it over the edge of the aquarium to keep it from being moved around by the flow of water. You can leave it like this to equalize water temperature.

A common fallacy

It has long been held that mixing small amounts of tank water with that in the bag will enable the fish to become accustomed to small changes in water chemistry. This is a pointless exercise as it takes a fish days, not minutes or hours, to adjust to such changes.

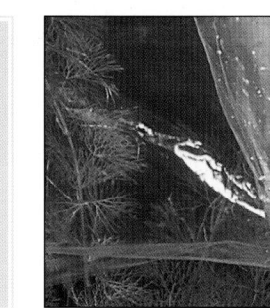

4 When the temperatures have equalized, release the fish gently into the tank. Do not just tip the bag upside down. Turn it gently onto its side and hold the top open with one hand while slowly upending the bottom to encourage the fish to swim out.

The furnished tank with your first fish

Having released your fish, quietly and carefully replace the condensation tray and hood. Switch on the light. Finally, make yourself a cup of tea or coffee, sit back, and admire your handiwork.

Do not feed the fish right away; give them a chance to settle down. Offer a first feed a few hours after they have been introduced to the tank, and then only a very small amount – just a couple of flakes will do for small fish. Do not be tempted to overfeed at this point or you will overload the whole system.

At first, the fish will take cover in the plants, but it will be only a matter of minutes before they come out to investigate their new home.

When closing the hood, do not let it bang shut as this will frighten the fish.

At first, the fish will show poor color; this is quite normal, as they are unsure of their surroundings. As they gain confidence, their colors will improve.

Keep a check on the temperature, but do not get paranoid about it. Remember, a fluctuation of one or two degrees is acceptable.

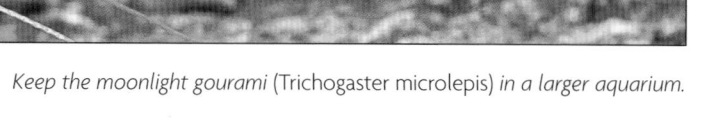

Keep the moonlight gourami (Trichogaster microlepis) *in a larger aquarium.*

Part Two:

Options and continuing care

In this part of the book, we start by examining some alternative filtration options. Filtration systems are many and various, cheap and expensive. We chose a simple and effective internal power filter for our aquarium, but you may wish to consider others. On the following pages you will see a selection of air-operated filters and those powered by electric pumps, all of which are suited to a community aquarium.

We also look in a bit more detail at tank decorations and aquarium plants. This will give you some further choices if you cannot find the plant species we have used in our setup. A small array of starter fish will help you decide which to introduce to your aquarium first.

Unexpected events can always occur in an aquarium – some happy, some not. Fish breed, so what do you do if you suddenly find a brood of guppies in the tank? A short section on breeding will provide you with the solution. Similarly, what is the answer to a fish that has become covered in small white spots? Look in the health section for guidance.

Above all, we take a look at maintaining the aquarium that you have so carefully set up. It is impossible to stress too strongly the importance of carrying out thorough, regular maintenance. Remembering to replenish stocks of used items, such as filter floss, or to keep spares may not seem necessary, but if a heater fails suddenly, you may not be able to buy a new one immediately.

Setting up your first tank is a challenge, but the effort is worthwhile when it culminates in a happy, healthy aquarium. Fishkeeping is a sociable hobby and talking to people about one's fish is half the fun, so enjoy it.

Using an external power filter

Several companies manufacture external power filters. These units vary in size and design and you need to choose one that is suitable for your particular aquarium. In theory, the unit should turn over the water in the aquarium twice an hour. In practice, it is usually slightly less than this, as the debris collecting in the canister reduces the water flow. The flow rate is normally given on the filter box, in either liters or gallons per hour.

Some units have the inlet and outlet at the top; others have the inlet at the base of the canister and the outlet at the top. The principle is the same for both. Water flows from the aquarium, is drawn through the filter medium, and is then pumped back into the tank. The main advantages of this system are that it does not take up valuable space in the aquarium, is easy to service, and is both efficient and versatile. The disadvantage is cost; external power filters are more expensive than other forms of filtration, but what price the lives of your fish?

External power filters are much larger than internal filters and can therefore accommodate more media for beneficial bacteria to colonize. Being located outside the aquarium, they are also easier to service. Most are supplied with shut-off taps. When these are closed, you can uncouple the filter unit and take it to the sink for cleaning. When cleaning, remember to rinse the filter media (the foam pad and porous pellets) with warm water to avoid killing off the bacteria. You can throw away the messiest bits of filter floss and replace them with fresh pieces.

Anatomy of an external filter

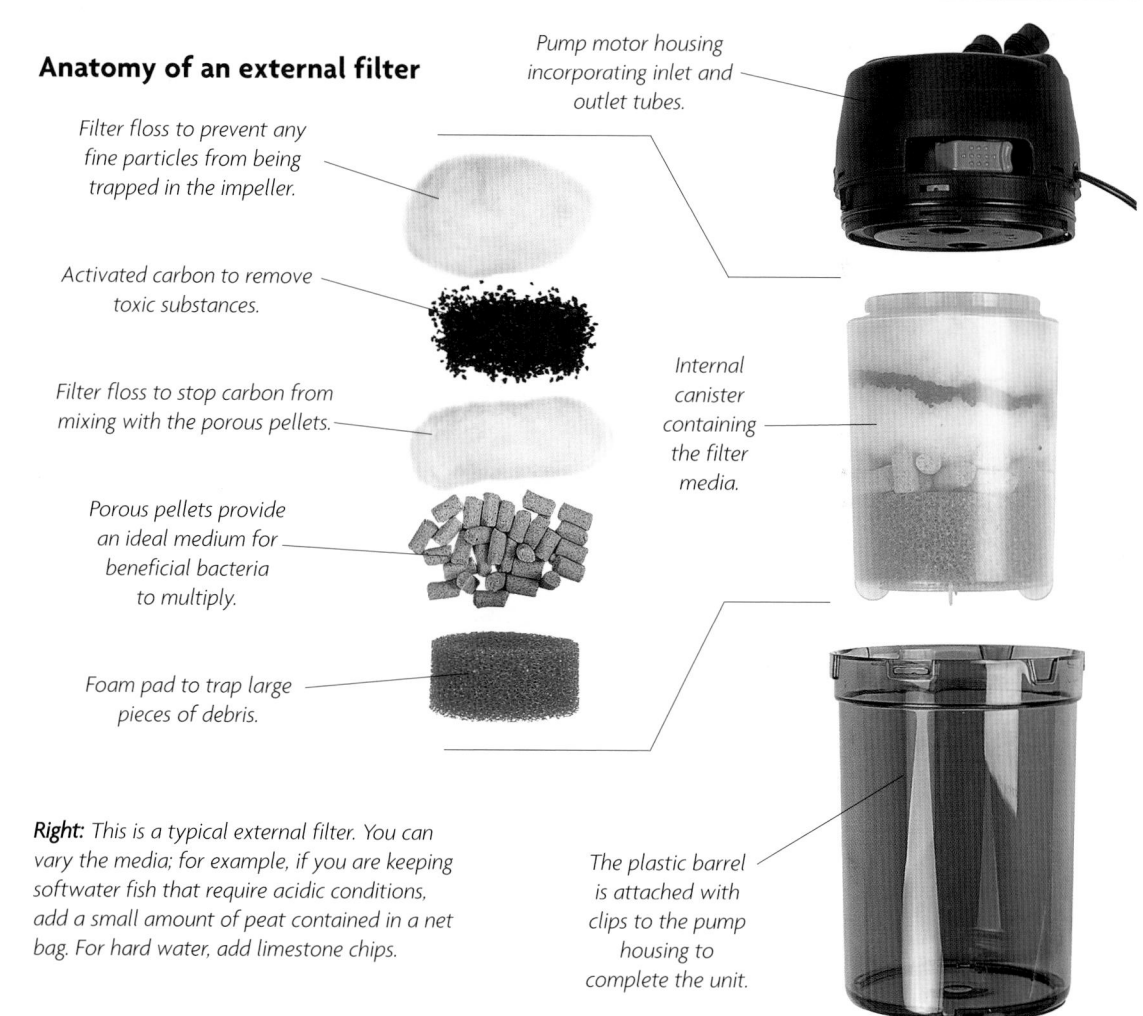

Filter floss to prevent any fine particles from being trapped in the impeller.

Activated carbon to remove toxic substances.

Filter floss to stop carbon from mixing with the porous pellets.

Porous pellets provide an ideal medium for beneficial bacteria to multiply.

Foam pad to trap large pieces of debris.

Pump motor housing incorporating inlet and outlet tubes.

Internal canister containing the filter media.

The plastic barrel is attached with clips to the pump housing to complete the unit.

Right: This is a typical external filter. You can vary the media; for example, if you are keeping softwater fish that require acidic conditions, add a small amount of peat contained in a net bag. For hard water, add limestone chips.

Above: If there are glass bars all around the top of the tank, slide the intake pipe through the access hole at the rear corner. Suction cups hold the pipes in position.

Place the intake basket just above the substrate (it looks higher here because there is no substrate). Then, if the worst happens and a pipe comes loose, all the water will not siphon out of the tank. A small amount will be left for the fish to survive in.

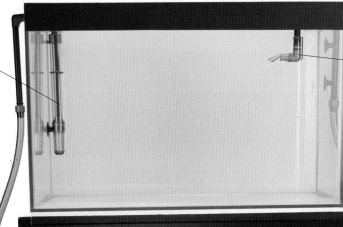

Place the return so that it is at, slightly above, or very slightly below the water surface. Here it is shown lower down for photographic purposes, or it would be hidden behind the black trim on the front of the aquarium.

Above: You can use suction cups to attach the rigid plastic part of the return pipe to the outer surface of the glass so that it reaches over the glass bars around the top of the tank.

Cut the inlet and outlet pipes to a suitable length to keep things neat.

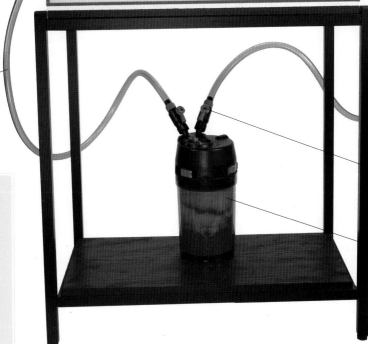

Taps allow the canister to be disconnected for maintenance without spilling water everywhere.

The most obvious place to put the external power filter is below the tank. If you have a cabinet, it can sit in there, but make sure there is a free flow of air around it, as the motor can overheat in confined spaces.

External filters are also biological

Remember that, although often sold as a mechanical filter (one that traps the debris outside the tank), once mature, an external power filter is also a biological filter with bacteria that break down the ammonia and nitrites in the same way as an undergravel or internal filter. You need to maintain your bacterial colonies when cleaning the filter to ensure its efficiency as a biological filter.

There are several other forms of filter systems. Each has its good and bad points and some are more suited to specific uses, such as quarantine or breeding tanks, than for community aquariums.

Undergravel filters

These consist of a single perforated plate – or several interlocking perforated plates – that completely covers the base glass of the aquarium. In one or both rear corners is an uplift tube. To power it, pass an airstone attached to a length of airline down the tube, or fit an air line to the base of the tube, depending on the design of the filter system. Then cover the plates with a layer of gravel, which will act as the filter bed. For the most efficient operation, the layer should be of an even thickness.

When the air supply is switched on, a stream of bubbles rises in the uplift tube, raising the column of water. To replace the displaced water, more is drawn through the perforated plates and through the gravel. The flow of oxygenated water through the gravel encourages beneficial bacteria to live in it, thereby turning a mechanical filter into a biological one as well.

To create a faster flow of water through the system, fit an electrically powered pump – or powerhead – on the top of the uplift tube. This is particularly useful for fish that naturally live in turbulent waters.

Never turn off this type of filter, as the bacteria will very quickly die if their oxygen supply is cut off and the tank will no longer be clean.

Installing an undergravel filter

Left: Position the filter plates so that they cover the complete base of the tank. Put them in place before you add any gravel, so that there is a free flow of water in the space below them.

Left: Now assemble the uplift tubes and slot them into position in a rear corner of the tank. Attach air lines and airstones as recommended by the manufacturer.

Left: Finally, add the well-washed substrate, making sure that it covers the entire filter plate. An even layer is far more efficient than banked substrate.

Above: In the finished aquarium, careful placement of the plants and hard decor will conceal the uplift tubes, but do make sure that the decor does not prevent the flow of water around the aquarium.

Box filters

These small, internal, air-powered filters are useful in breeding and quarantine tanks. Designs vary, but the basic principle remains the same. Assemble the filter according to the manufacturer's instructions. Fill the canister with a layer of gravel or marbles to weight it down, or the whole thing floats when you turn on the air supply. Then add a thin layer of filter floss, followed by some activated carbon, and finally another thin layer of filter floss. Switch on the air supply and the filter is ready. If you need to set up one of these in a hurry, just use gravel as the filter medium. The gravel will be colonized by bacteria and will act as a filter bed, just as it does with an undergravel system. Many aquarists keep one of these little filters up and running in one of their tanks so that it is always ready for use (matured) should they need to set up a small breeding tank in a hurry.

Air pumps

These are available in a variety of sizes, from single outlet units to twin and multiple outlet pumps. There are two basic forms: the diaphragm pump, which is both cheaper and more readily available, although a little noisy if not serviced regularly, and the piston pump, a more expensive but quieter option. See what your dealer has to offer and buy one to suit your pocketbook and your aquarium.

Before you buy a pump, you must decide what you need it for. If it is to run the undergravel filter, a single outlet would do, but do not buy the smallest one. Choose one that is slightly larger, because there will be times when you need an air supply, perhaps to aerate water to get rid of chlorine, to run a box filter in a quarantine tank, to operate a cleaner to remove debris from the gravel, to add an ornament – the list goes on. As you can see, even if you are running aquarium that does not need an air supply, it is still worth buying an air pump because you can be sure that you will need it sooner or later, and usually when the stores are closed!

An external power filter

This type of power filter hangs over the tank glass. Water is drawn up by an impeller into the unit and cascades back into the aquarium over a plastic chute, having first passed through a floss bag filled with activated charcoal and then through a pad of filter foam. This makes an excellent alternative to internal power filters, provided your hood can accommodate it. This type of filter is best used on a tank in a display cabinet, where you can hide it from view – but make sure there is a good flow of air through the cabinet to prevent the motor from overheating. The photograph below shows the filter with the cover removed and the floss bag filled with carbon pulled up into view.

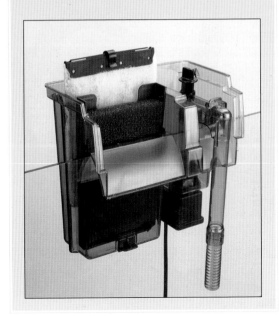

Other types of tank decoration

If you prefer not to add rocks and wood to the aquarium, there are some artificial alternatives. Rocklike structures are available in various shapes and sizes that you can use to create instant rock walls, arches, etc. Artificial wood can look very realistic, especially when it is combined with real plants. The advantages of these types of tank decor are that they do not need any preparation (other than a quick wash to remove any dust) and they will not affect the water quality. On the other hand, they are not as individual as natural rocks and wood and you might find that your friend down the road has exactly the same tank decor as you. If you do decide to use artificial decor, buy all the pieces of, say, wood from the same manufacturer, as each one seems to have its own color scheme and surface texture. Mixing different products can look very unnatural.

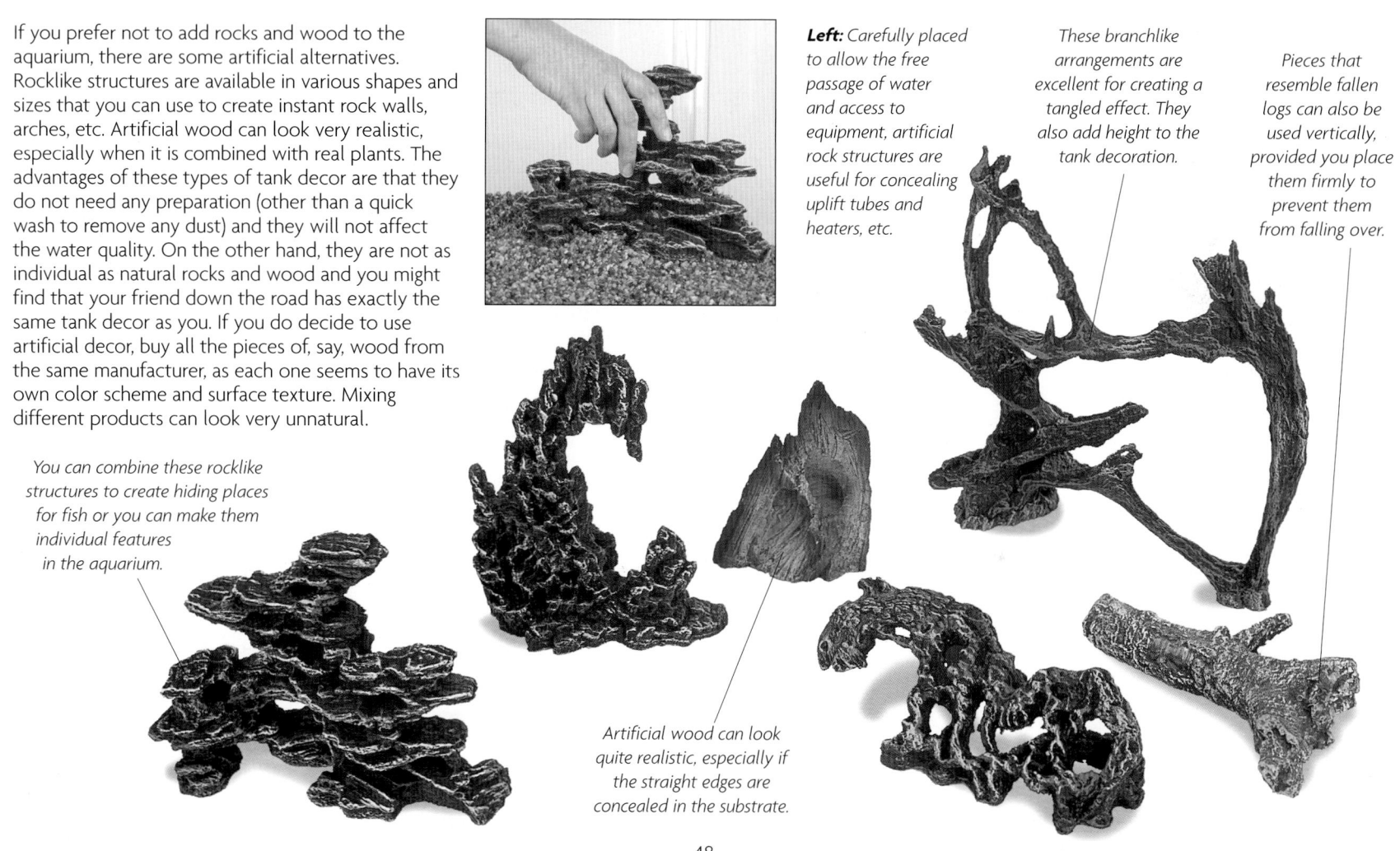

Left: Carefully placed to allow the free passage of water and access to equipment, artificial rock structures are useful for concealing uplift tubes and heaters, etc.

These branchlike arrangements are excellent for creating a tangled effect. They also add height to the tank decoration.

Pieces that resemble fallen logs can also be used vertically, provided you place them firmly to prevent them from falling over.

You can combine these rocklike structures to create hiding places for fish or you can make them individual features in the aquarium.

Artificial wood can look quite realistic, especially if the straight edges are concealed in the substrate.

Left: *Air-operated ornaments can provide movement in the aquarium. Some have parts that fill with air, then lift up to release a large bubble; young children are captivated by these! Others release a continuous stream of small bubbles.*

Of course, a market has developed for novelties in the aquarium and whether or not you include these is purely a matter of personal choice. If they are sold by one of the major manufacturers, you can be sure that they do not incorporate any toxic substances that could harm your fish. Avoid buying cheap plastic novelties of dubious origin, as these may have been manufactured from substances that could harm your fish. Whether you are drawn to sunken galleons and divers, underwater cities, or cartoon fish, you will find something suitable. Some items, such as the diver shown here, are air powered. Simply attach an air line to the model and connect it to an air pump. The stream of bubbles rising to the surface not only lends a realistic appearance to the diver, but also helps to agitate the water surface, thus improving the exchange of gases to and from the aquarium.

Sunken buildings and galleons can be effectively combined with some of the picture backgrounds of sunken cities.

Make sure your pump can power another item before you buy an air-operated model such as this diver.

Very young children delight in colorful, cartoonlike ornaments such as these.

There are many aquatic plants available and the final choice is up to you. Select those that are suited to aquatic life and not ones that are best grown as houseplants because, although these will live for a few weeks underwater, they will eventually rot. The plants shown on the next few pages are all suited to aquatic life. Plastic plants are another option and there is nothing wrong with using these if you wish.

Ludwigia is a versatile plant that, once established, grows prolifically. Keep it under control by regular pruning. You can plant the prunings in the tank.

Water wisteria (Hygrophila difformis) requires good light to maintain vigorous growth, or it becomes very long and lanky. A good plant for the background.

Taking cuttings of aquarium plants

Some cuttings of popular aquarium plants are collected from the wild during the dry season in the tropical regions in which they grow. During this time, the plants have woody stems and may flower, and the leaf shapes differ from the submersed form. It is easy to tell if the plants have been growing out of water, or emersed; hold the base of the stem and the plant will remain upright. If you try this with a plant grown underwater, it will flop over because the water normally holds it up. You can use these woody cuttings to create underwater plants for your aquarium. Plant them in a spare tank full of water and

wait. Remove the leaves as they die off and, after a short time, shoots appear from some leaf joints. Cut off these underwater growths and plant them as normal cuttings. What you have done is to repeat the normal cycle of the plant in the wild and provide it with a sudden rainy season. It has responded by producing its underwater leaves that enable it to survive. These are often softer and of a different shape and color than its emersed leaves. Many aquarium plants are now mist-propagated to prevent undue pressures on wild stocks. They may shed a few leaves when submerged, but this is quite natural.

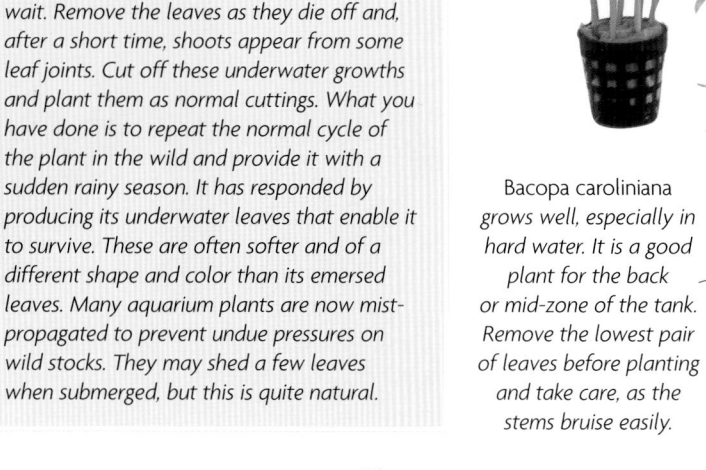

Bacopa caroliniana grows well, especially in hard water. It is a good plant for the back or mid-zone of the tank. Remove the lowest pair of leaves before planting and take care, as the stems bruise easily.

Right: *Creating this type of aquarium requires careful planning. A broad-leaved rooted plant forms the focal point here, while a variety of species available as cuttings provide other shapes and colors.*

Plants for a tropical freshwater aquarium

Anubias nana *(growing on wood)*

Bacopa *sp., including* B. caroliniana

Cabomba caroliniana *(the standard green cabomba)*

Ceratopsis thalictroides *(Indian fern, a floating plant that can also be planted in the substrate)*

Cryptocoryne *sp. including* C. ciliata *(50cm/20in),* C. willissii *(13-20 cm/5-8 in)* and C. wendtii *(5-10 cm/2-4 in)*

Echinodorus martii *(ruffled Amazon sword),* E. paniculatus *and* E. tennellus *(Amazon swordplant)*

Hygrophila polysperma *and* H. corymbosa *(willow leaf hygrophila)*

Limnophila aquatica *(giant ambulia)*

Ludwigia mullertii *(red ludwigia)* L. repens *and* L. palustris

Microsorium pteropus *(Java fern – growing on wood)*

Hygrophila difformis *(water wisteria)*

Vallisneria spiralis *(straight vallis)*

Vallisneria tortifolia *(twisted vallis)*

Vesicularia dubyana *(Java moss)*

Rotala indica *has greenish pink leaves and contrasts well with the bright green plants. It grows well, quickly forming a large thicket that fish delight in hiding and spawning in.*

Cabomba *will quickly break up in turbulent water. Plant it in a quiet, well-lit spot and it will flourish.*

There are several species of Ludwigia; some have green leaves, others reddish leaves. The red ones require more light than the green.

Use rooted plants to create a focal point in your aquarium. Amazon swordplants are prime examples of this; in our tank there is room for only a single specimen because the majority of them grow large. Vallis, both straight and twisted, are ideal for dense plantings, while *Cryptocoryne* is normally regarded as a carpeting plant, sending out runners to colonize the tank. But beware, some *Cryptocoryne* are large plants; if you want a carpet, choose the low-growing ones. When planting rooted plants, you will see a white area at the base that shows how deep in the substrate the plant was growing. You should plant them with this area just covered.

When buying your Cryptocoryne, check that it has no decaying leaves or stems, as this can quickly spread to the crown and destroy the plant. Look for healthy specimens such as this.

Twisted vallis gets its name from its attractive twisted leaves. It tends not to grow as tall as straight vallis. Propagate by runners.

Straight vallis is tall, with fairly brittle leaves that snap easily. You may be misled by its scientific name, Vallisneria spiralis. The "spiralis" refers to the flower stems that spiral upward.

Leaf shapes vary in species of Amazon swordplants. Use those with large, leaves to create shady areas in the aquarium.

The broad-leaved Amazon swordplant (Echinodorus paniculatus) tolerates a range of water conditions including hard alkaline water.

Attaching a plant to wood

Some plants, such as this Java fern, will grow attached to a piece of wood. This is most useful when you are trying to create height in an aquarium or if you are keeping fish that dig in the substrate.

1 You will need a piece of wood, some dark nylon thread, a pair of sharp scissors, and a healthy-looking piece of Java fern.

Best grown in subdued light, Java fern can develop clear patches on the leaves in bright conditions; these may later turn brown.

2 Cut a length of thread and wind it across the rhizome between the leaves of the fern. Lay the rhizome at a convenient place on the wood – there will be one place where it sits quite naturally – and gently tie off the thread around the wood. Be very careful not to pull too tightly or you will cut into, or even through, the rhizome. Trim the long ends of the thread. The plant is now ready for your tank.

Once established in the aquarium, the fine roots spread and take hold of the wood. It can take several months for it to establish itself properly.

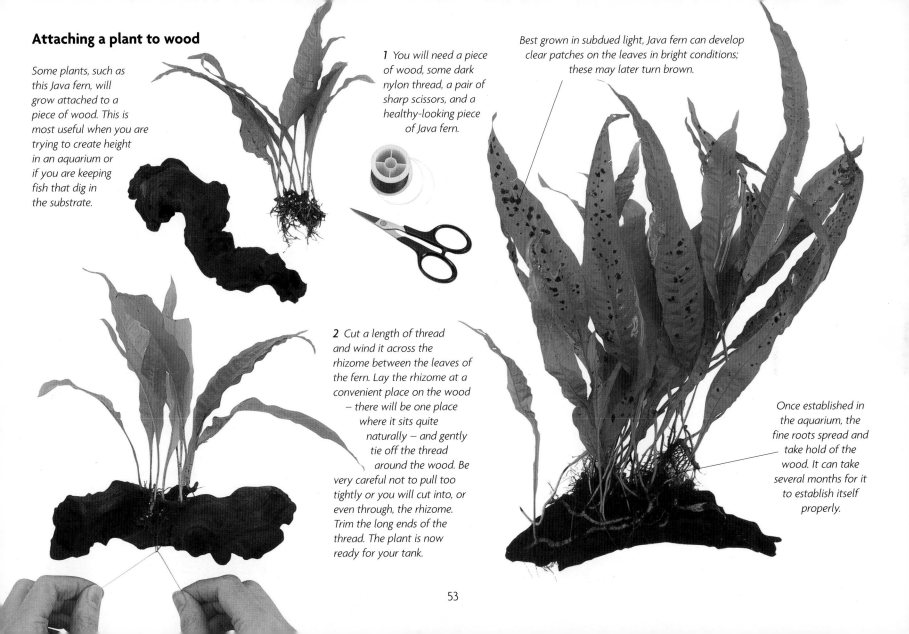

53

Using plastic plants in the aquarium

These days, you can choose from a wide range of very realistic plastic plants. They are not to everyone's taste, but they do have their uses, especially if you have fish that are continually uprooting plants. They are easy to position; just sink the tray at the base of the plant into the gravel to hold it in place. You can also pull plastic plants apart and fit them back together again to lengthen or shorten them. Best of all, if they get covered in algae, you can take them out and scrub them clean. On the other hand, plastic plants are inert so they will do nothing to assist in the removal of nitrates from the tank as real plants would. It is essential, therefore, that you pay particular attention to regular water changes and the efficiency of your filtration system. Plastic plants are probably best used in conjunction with a few real ones.

Right: To achieve a thicket of plants, choose two or three of the same type, but vary the heights. This is easy to do. Just split the stems and add or remove sections until you have a stem of the desired length.

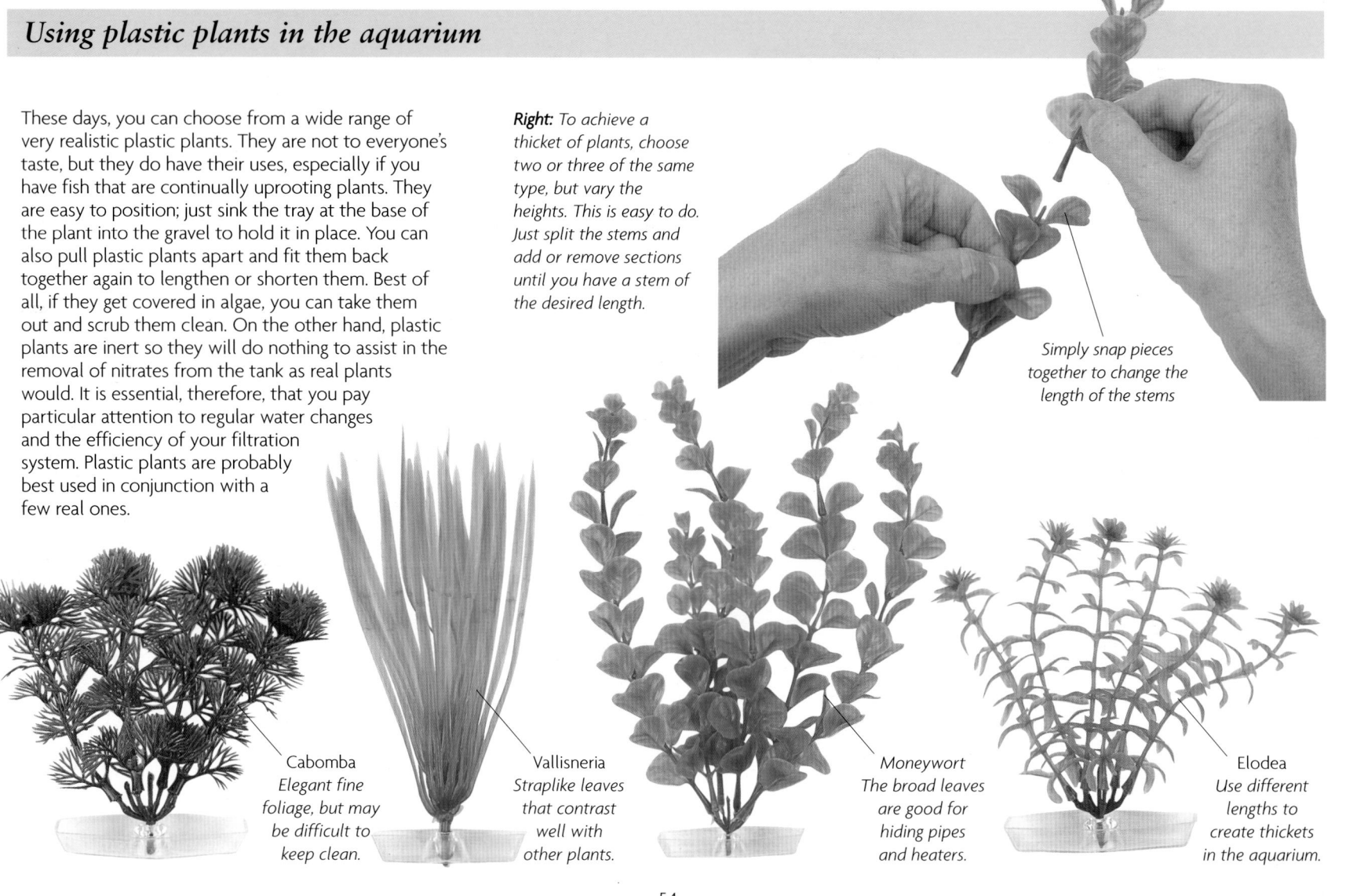

Simply snap pieces together to change the length of the stems

Cabomba
Elegant fine foliage, but may be difficult to keep clean.

Vallisneria
Straplike leaves that contrast well with other plants.

Moneywort
The broad leaves are good for hiding pipes and heaters.

Elodea
Use different lengths to create thickets in the aquarium.

54

Above: *Plastic plants are easy to position in the aquarium. Simply hold the plant at the base and push it firmly into the substrate so that it cannot be seen.*

Preparing plastic plants

When you remove plastic plants from the wrapping, some of them may be kinked and bent into strange shapes. Lay them out in a warm place for several hours so that the plastic becomes more pliable. They will look more natural and it will be easier to judge their full height and shape before "planting" them in the aquarium.

Fabric plants

Depending on the type of effect you wish to create in your aquarium, some retailers offer fabric plants and leaves for aquarium use. These can be bent into realistic shapes, but their main drawback is that they are not artificial aquarium plants, but artificial potted plants. The choice is yours.

Above: *Fill the clear plastic trough at the base with gravel to prevent the plant from floating. An advantage of plastic plants is that you can position them before filling the tank with water.*

Above: *If you choose plastic plants with care, you can create a pleasing display and hide heaters and filter pipes from view. Select plants that complement each other, both in leaf shape and color, but use reds sparingly as they can really stand out and may detract from the fish.*

A selection of fish for your first aquarium

The first fish that you add to your aquarium need to be hardy creatures, as they will have to cope with fluctuations in water quality and feeding regimes while you are learning how to keep them fit and healthy. The fish featured on the next few pages are all suited to this purpose, and will live in water that is slightly soft to slightly hard, slightly acidic to slightly alkaline, and with a temperature of 23-24°C (73-75°F). However, that does not mean you have to keep all of them! Choose four to six fish, but not all different ones. Find out whether they are schooling fish and if so, buy a small group of them. If they like to live in pairs, buy a pair. By taking their lifestyles into consideration, you will help the fish to feel settled and at ease and thus more able to cope with any minor discrepancies in water quality or feeding. Remember that the fish you choose will be with you for quite some time, so be sure you like them.

▼ Rosy barb – *Barbus conchonius*

These active schooling fish will tolerate a wide range of water conditions, provided you do not let the temperature rise above 23°C (73°F) for any length of time, or they become a bit lethargic. They will eat just about anything you offer and school happily and peacefully with other barbs. Being active fish, they do like some open water to swim in. The long-finned form is less robust and best avoided by novice fishkeepers.

A healthy fish shows good color and has no damaged fins.

▲ Cherry barb – *Barbus titteya*

The deep red color of the males is enough to make you want to keep these little fish, but do not buy only males; their color will be much better if they have some females to display to. They are tolerant of other species and a small school of four will add movement to the middle of the tank. They are easy to feed on basic flake food, but like some frozen daphnia or bloodworm in their diet. They like warmth and will sulk and go off their food if the temperature drops below 23°C (73°F) for any length of time.

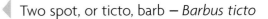

Two spot, or ticto, barb — *Barbus ticto*

You might walk straight past these fish in the store because they never look quite so colorful there, but take them home, offer them a diet that includes some green foods, and they will blossom. With their liking for green foods, the barbs are useful in a new tank as they will pick at some of the algae that forms. Buying four or five of these little fish should ensure that you have both sexes. They will swim happily around your tank, minding their own business.

White Cloud Mountain minnow — *Tanichthys albonubes*

Although small – they grow to only 4cm (1.6in) at most – white clouds are tough little fish that like cool conditions, so do not exceed the basic temperature of 23°C (73°F) for more than a few days. They are active and enjoy the company of their own kind. Provide them with some cover in the form of fine-leaved plants, such as cabomba. They will feed readily on flake foods, but to keep the attractive iridescent sheen on their bodies, include some frozen daphnia or bloodworm in their diet. If they settle into the tank and are happy, pairs can often be seen spawning over fine-leaved plants.

◀ Zebra danio – *Brachydanio rerio*

The zebra's popularity is probably due to its strikingly striped body. In good, mature specimens, the background color is a very deep blue, and the stripes are creamy gold, but do not expect to see this in the store, where the young fish may look a little pale. However, with a varied diet that includes some live or frozen and green foods, these small, schooling fish soon develop into good-quality adults. Keep a group of at least four fish to see them at their best.

▼ Coolie loach – *Pangio kuhlii*

At first, this bottom-dwelling fish that rummages in the substrate searching for food might look like a very skinny shoelace, but it is often the first to find any food that sinks to the bottom and, provided the food is small enough, it will eat it. Although it will live alone, buy two so that they can interact. Coolies are active by night, so feeding them just before your bedtime is a good idea, but this does not seem to stop them from coming out during the day as well.

Swordtail – *Xiphophorus helleri*

Swordtails can become quite large; a good female can grow to 12cm (4.7in) long. Males are slightly shorter in the body, but look longer because of the long extension (sword) on the bottom of their caudal fin. They will eat flake but also need algae and green foods to keep them healthy. Keep swordtails in pairs. They are live-bearers and may breed in the aquarium. A fully grown female may give birth to up to 80 small fry. Several color forms are available but the wild fish, such as the one shown here, is still a beautiful creature.

Platy – *Xiphophorus maculatus*

Platies are closely related to swordtails, but are much smaller. They are also live-bearers, but not as prolific as their larger cousins. In a newly set-up aquarium they are almost indispensable, as they are forever picking on algal growths and cleaning up the plant leaves without damaging the plants themselves. As you can imagine, they like green foods but should also be offered some flaked food. Several color forms are available, some with extended finnage. The latter are more difficult to keep than the standard form.

59

▲ Pearl gourami — *Trichogaster leeri*

There is no doubt that the pearl gourami is a stunning fish, but you do need to choose its tankmates with care, as some of them cannot resist the temptation to nibble at the mature male's long, flowing finnage. If you are starting up a larger tank, pearl gouramis are good fish to keep. Although they may spar with each other, they rarely pick on other fish. They like a tank with some plant cover so that they have a secure area to retire to. Feed them a varied diet that includes some frozen and live foods. Buy a pair; females have shorter finnage.

▼ Blue gourami — *Trichogaster trichopterus*

Blue gouramis are some of the best fish for novice aquarists because they are not in the least bit fussy about water conditions or food; if it fits into their mouths, they eat it. They are also easy to breed; indeed, a pair will often build a nest in a quiet corner of the community tank, but the fry do not usually survive because the other inmates treat them as a free lunch. Their only drawback can be that males often bicker with each other, but they rarely pick on other fish. Opaline and gold forms are also available.

▶ Kissing gourami — *Helostoma temmincki*

The kissing gourami is quite a large fish and thus suited to the larger community aquarium, but youngsters can be included in smaller tanks as algae eaters. They need a great deal of green food in their diet, so they are more than willing to go around your newly set-up tank grazing on the algae. But they cannot survive on this alone and need flake and frozen foods as well. The "kissing" act is a trial of strength and has nothing to do with passion. They are available in two naturally occurring color forms: pink and green.

▼ Bronze *Corydoras* — *Corydoras aeneus*

This tough but gentle little catfish will take just about everything you can throw at it and survive, but it deserves better. Catfish are often described as scavengers because they feed from the bottom, and while they will eat up any food that reaches the substrate, you must ensure that they are getting their fair share. One tablet of food dropped to the substrate each evening will keep a couple of Corydoras catfish fed. Do not expect them to eat everything on the substrate; you must clear away the debris when you do water changes.

Compatibility

Do not buy your first fish on a whim; they need to coexist harmoniously with future additions to the aquarium. Plan your full choice of fish, taking into account size, territorial needs, swimming levels, etc., and then pick the most robust of these to introduce first.

Foods and feeding

Just like any living thing, fish need food to survive and the only way they can get it is when you give it to them. In the wild they can swim upstream or downstream to where their preferred food is abundant, but in the confines of the aquarium, they have only what they are given. Always take the fish's natural diet into consideration and offer it the equivalent commercial food. A vast range of foods has been developed to cater to all types of fish needs and the array of packaging can be confusing, so it is best that we look at each type of food.

Below: *Frozen foods have become one of the mainstays of fishkeeping, being both clean and convenient to use. Most are available in foil packs; simply pop a cube of food out of the pack, thaw it, and feed it to the fish. The sizes and range of foods available cater to the needs of virtually every fish. They are an excellent food source and especially useful for bringing fish into condition for spawning. Below are (left to right) chopped mussel, bloodworm, and brine shrimp.*

Tablet foods
These are much like flake foods, but in another form. Some "stick" on the side of the tank and are ideal for midwater community fish. Sinking tablets benefit some of the bottom-dwelling fish.

Finely powdered fry foods
These are similar in formula to basic flake foods. All are useful, but beware: You can quickly pollute a tank by overfeeding.

Right: *Liquid fry foods for live-bearers and egg-layers contain the food in suspension.*

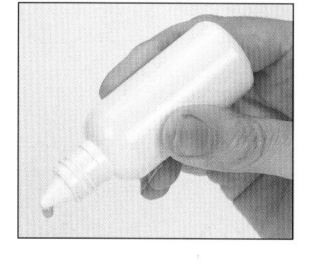

Floating food sticks
These are useful for feeding the larger barbs.

Freeze-dried foods
These are available as small cubes, here tubifex.

Freeze-dried foods
These are also sold as fine, loose food. Here: mosquito larvae.

Dried foods
These are available in various forms and can provide the staple diet for most fish. Offer them sparingly as, left uneaten, they can quickly pollute the aquarium. Flake foods are the most common form. They have been developed to accommodate the needs of herbivores and carnivores and also to enhance the color of fish.

Sinking granules
These are for suitable for bottom-dwelling catfish.

How much to feed your fish

Feeding your fish once a day is fine. A hungry (but not starving) fish is a healthy fish. With dried and frozen foods, feed only what the fish will consume in about 15 minutes. The rules are different for herbivores; you can leave the green food in the tank until the next feeding, but remove the old food before offering fresh supplies. Start with small amounts, such as a small pinch of flake, one or two tablets or a single lettuce leaf, and increase or decrease the amount as necessary.

When you feed the fish will depend on the fish you are keeping. Some like to come out at dawn and dusk, while others will feed during the day. Fortunately for us, fish obligingly change some of their feeding habits in the confines of the aquarium, and will come out as soon as they sense food. Just be sure to check that food is reaching all the fish.

Fish benefit greatly from variety in their diet. Use dried food as a basis, but offer some frozen or live foods once or twice a week. Live and frozen foods help to maintain the sheen on the body of your fish and to grow young fish into healthy adults.

Mosquito larvae

One live food that you can get free is mosquito larvae. Just leave a bucket of water outdoors and it will soon have the larvae in it. These small black wiggly creatures make excellent fish food. Net them from the bucket and feed them to your fish.

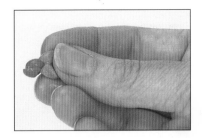

Right: Squeeze the frozen pea between your finger and thumb to release the inner seed. Discard the seed coats because fish tend to get trapped in them. Feed sparingly and remove uneaten peas daily. Cut down on the amount you offer until you do not have to remove any.

Lettuce leaves
"Plant" these in the substrate for the fish to graze on. Left to float, the fish usually ignore them.

Below: There are a number of green foods that you can feed to herbivorous fish. Offer them regularly and the fish will leave your plants alone. Remove any uneaten leaves or slices before they start to rot, and replace them with fresh supplies.

Left: *Daphnia and bloodworm are live foods that are sometimes available in aquatic outlets. Daphnia (also known as water fleas — but they will not hop all over you so don't panic!) is well suited to small fish. Larger fish relish bloodworm (midge larvae of an intense red color). Both daphnia and bloodworm are sold in small plastic bags full of water. Strain the contents through a fine net so that you only feed the daphnia or bloodworm to the fish. Do not put the water into the aquarium. Bloodworm is sometimes sold "dry," packed in damp paper. It is a much better value when sold this way.*

Frozen peas
These are taken by many fish, except for the strict herbivores.

Zucchini and potato
Parboil slices until they are soft but will not break up. May also be fed uncooked.

Although you may not set out with any intention of breeding your fish, there is every chance that if conditions are to their liking, they will breed. If this happens, the question is, what do you do next?

The tropical species you are keeping fall into two groups: live-bearers and egg-layers. The first young fish you are likely to encounter in the community aquarium are the young of live-bearing fishes.

Live-bearers

As their name suggests, these fish give birth to fully formed live young. They are usually quite large and the brood is a manageable size. Being larger than the fry that hatch from eggs, they have a reasonable chance of survival in the community tank, but some will fall prey to the other fish. They are able to nibble at the edge of flake food and will pick at algae on plants. To help feed them, you can crumble some flake food or add one of the liquid suspension foods for live-bearers (see page 62). Be extremely careful not to overdo the liquid food, as it can quickly pollute the aquarium. If in doubt, put two or three drops onto a teaspoon and wash it off the spoon in the aquarium.

You also need to consider that these extra bodies, however small now, will grow and thus increase your stock levels beyond the capacity of the aquarium and its life-support system (the filter). In short, you will need another tank. A tank measuring 45 x 25 x 25 cm (18 x 10 x 10 in) makes a useful rearing tank. And when it is not being used for this purpose, it makes an ideal emergency quarantine tank. Set up the tank as normal. Partially fill it with water from

the main aquarium and add a small amount of fresh water. (Top off the main tank with fresh water as if you were doing a water change.) In this way, you have combined aged water from the main tank with a little fresh and can safely net and transfer the youngsters to the rearing tank without having to wait for the water to age; in effect, you have done a water change on both tanks. Be careful with the level of feeding; keep it low until the filter has had a chance to build up enough bacteria to cope. The

amount of time fry spend in rearing tanks depends on their growth rate. Do not put them with other fish until they are large enough not to be eaten. If you have too many fry, give them to friends or take them to your local aquarium club or shop.

Below: Female platies often give birth in the aquarium. They seek out a quiet place, frequently near the water surface in the shelter of plants, and this gives the fry a chance to escape predation.

Egg-layers

These fish are a little more difficult to deal with. Although some species will spawn in the community aquarium, few succeed in raising a brood because the other inmates consider the eggs and fry to be free meals. It is far better to set up a breeding tank with whatever the fish require (fine-leaved plants, caves, slate, etc.), and spawn the fish in this. Depending on species – and you will need to find out about the fish you are intending to spawn – you should remove one or both parents after spawning and return them to the main aquarium, or leave them to tend the eggs and subsequent fry.

Conditioning the parents is important. Again, investigate the species you are keeping and feed them on the correct foods to bring them into spawning condition before you try to breed them.

Feeding the fry of egg-layers is fraught with problems. Sometimes the fry are so tiny that they will eat only infusoria, tiny microscopic creatures that you have to culture. Others are slightly larger and need newly hatched brine shrimp. For these you can buy brine shrimp eggs to hatch in saline water. Fortunately, some fry – but by no means all – will take some of the fine commercial live-bearer fry foods that are available in either liquid or powder form. Other fry will require green foods in the form of algae, frozen peas, and lettuce leaves (see pages 62–63).

Left: If well fed and healthy, there is nothing to stop a pair of cherry barbs (Barbus titteya) from spawning among fine-leaved plants in the community aquarium. If you can retrieve the egg-filled plant before the other fish in the aquarium eat the eggs, remove it and place it in a specially set up breeding tank (page 67). You can safely hatch and rear the fry in this tank.

Raising fry successfully

Whichever kind of fish you are breeding, cleanliness is all-important. Eggs can quickly develop a fungus if conditions are poor in the aquarium or the eggs are infertile, and tiny fry can contract bacterial infections in dirty conditions.

Another cause of losses is starvation, either because you do not have food ready when the fry need it or because you are feeding foods that are simply too large for the fry to eat. It does not matter how much food you regularly put into the tank; if it is the wrong size or offered at the wrong time, the fish will starve. More fish are probably lost for these reasons than for any other.

Broods can vary in size. Some fish produce 10 or 12 young; others produce thousands. You cannot hope to raise every fish in a large brood, so it is better to settle for raising 50 healthy adults than 1,000 small stunted specimens. Fish do not just need food to grow, they also need space, and very few of us have enough room to raise fry in large numbers.

Left: Some fish, such as this whiptail catfish, lay eggs on flat surfaces – here, the tank glass. This male fish is guarding the eggs against other fish in the tank.

It is difficult to admit, but most of the problems that occur in a fish tank are up to us. The major reason for things going wrong is poor water quality because we forget or delay doing something about it. This is when you begin to see the benefit of keeping an aquarium log. Get yourself a notebook and each time you do something to your tank, write down the date and what you did, because it is very easy to forget. Did you do the water change last week or was it the week before? Also note down observations such as behavior patterns, as any change may alert you to a potential problem or event. The log helps to get you into the habit of looking, seeing what you are looking at, and acting on it.

Keeping the water in good condition is the key to successful fishkeeping. It means that you must do regular water changes and ensure that your filtration system is working properly. Your fish will indicate that there may be a potential problem. If they hang near the surface, the chances are that oxygen levels are low. Check the temperature and the flow from your filter, and correct as necessary. Remember that during hot summer months, the temperature can rise above normal levels even when the thermostat has switched your heater off. At such times, a water change and increasing the water flow from your filter or adding an airstone to increase turbulence at the water surface will help.

Another common problem is stress caused by incompatible tankmates or poor conditions. This can weaken a fish so that it becomes an easy target for illness. Choose your fish with care.

Buying healthy fish

Fish travel long distances to get to our tanks. They may have been bred on farms in the Far East, then caught and transported to packing stations, where they are repacked for air shipment to us. Upon arrival, they are driven to a wholesaler, who unpacks them and rests them before they go on sale to retailers. Again they are packed and transported to the retail outlet, where they are finally unpacked, rested, and put on sale. What happens when we buy them? They are packed, yet again, and taken home by us. All this can be stressful and, despite all the best endeavors at each stage of the process, some fish will fall ill and some will perish.

Do not be surprised if you see tanks in quarantine at your local shop or signs that say something like "New arrivals, not for sale yet." This is your retailer looking after his stock, and a sign of a good shop.

When you go out to buy your fish, check to see that they are active and behaving normally. For example, schooling fish should be swimming around with their fins held out, whereas bottom-dwelling species will be searching around on the substrate for morsels of food. Avoid fish with split fins or badly damaged barbels, as both can be sites of potential secondary fungal or bacterial infection. Avoid fish with pinched-looking bellies or sunken eyes; they may not be feeding properly or may have internal parasites.

To quarantine or not to quarantine?

This is always a problem for novices because you have only one tank. When you start out, you have to

Left: Healthy fish sell themselves. They parade around the aquarium, almost inviting you to buy them and take them home. A fish such as this barb is a credit to the aquatic dealer who has successfully brought it through the final stages of transportation before putting it on sale. You can buy a fish like this with confidence.

rely on your retailer providing you with quality fish. Later on, you may decide to set up a quarantine tank that also doubles as a breeding tank – but that is some way down the line.

For many problems, quarantining is not an option. Take white spot. This little parasite's life cycle includes a free-swimming stage, when it is most susceptible to treatment. If you quarantined the fish with the spots, you would cure them, but there would still be cysts in the main tank. By treating the main tank, you should target both fish and cysts. For other problems, quarantining is effective. For instance, fish with a severe case of fungus have to be treated twice a day and this is easier to deal with in a separate tank.

A quarantine tank should be of a suitable size for the fish being treated. It should have either a bare base or a fine covering of sand or gravel, a cave or two if the fish needs shelter, and one or two potted plants to aid seclusion. Keeping the fish in a totally bare tank can cause more stress and aggravation, rather than alleviate the problem. A corner filter, sponge filter, or small internal power filter will help to keep the water sweet. And do not forget a cover, such as a condensation tray or hood.

Right: If your main aquarium is on a stand, you can use the bottom shelf for a quarantine tank. If not, you need to find a quiet place for it. To make the fish feel safe and secure, add a small amount of decor, or they will become frightened and stressed. To help calm the fish, you can cover the front of the tank with a sheet of brown paper or some dark cloth, removing part of it two or three times a day to check on the progress of the treatment. Be sure to keep quarantine tanks clean. Remember that these tanks can also be used as emergency rearing tanks if your fish suddenly produce a brood in the community aquarium.

A treatment/quarantine tank

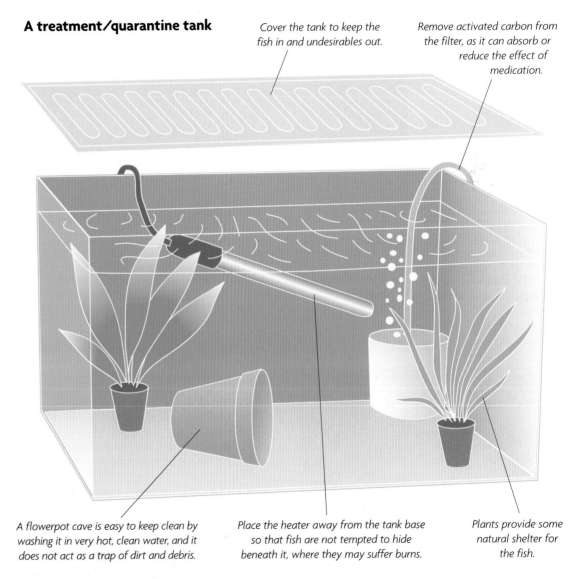

Cover the tank to keep the fish in and undesirables out.

Remove activated carbon from the filter, as it can absorb or reduce the effect of medication.

A flowerpot cave is easy to keep clean by washing it in very hot, clean water, and it does not act as a trap of dirt and debris.

Place the heater away from the tank base so that fish are not tempted to hide beneath it, where they may suffer burns.

Plants provide some natural shelter for the fish.

The problems described on these pages are by no means the only ones that can occur in an aquarium, but they are the main ones that you are likely to encounter. All are easily treated, provided they are caught early – a key factor in keeping your aquarium healthy. Some will respond to a simple water change; others will need medication. Before you buy any medication, make sure you have diagnosed the problem correctly – do not guess; treating with the wrong product will not cure the problem. And give the medication time to work. It is not instant; some take several days. Certain medications can be unsuitable for some fish species, so read the label carefully before buying a product and, if in doubt, ask. The effectiveness of medications deteriorates with time, so it is best to buy them as you need them. Never overdose. Follow all the instructions, or the result can be fatal. And above all, never mix medications; a lethal concoction can result.

White spot
Caused by a parasite, *Ichthyophthirius multifiliis*, these small creatures are noticeable at the stage when they appear as small white spots on the body and fins of their host. They spend time under the skin of the fish until they mature, when they break out and fall to the bottom of the aquarium and form cysts. Within each cyst, cell division produces over 1,000 new parasites. When the cyst ruptures, they break out to infect a new host. It is during this free-swimming stage that white spot can be effectively treated. Treat the whole tank using a brand-name white spot cure and follow the instructions carefully.

Fungus
Fungus is a secondary infection that gets into wounds when the body mucus has been damaged by injury, environmental factors, or parasites. (One fish picking at another's fins is a prime cause.) It manifests itself as fluffy cotton wool-like growths on the body and/or fins. For minor outbreaks, spot-treat the site of infection with a commercially available aquarium fungicide. For major outbreaks, treat the whole tank. Above all, remedy the cause.

Above: To treat this advanced outbreak of fungus on a Corydoras rabauti, *carefully "paint" the affected area with a soft, small paintbrush dipped in the medication. You may need to repeat this daily until the fungus lifts off. Then keep the wound clean until it heals.*

Left: *A typical outbreak of white spot, as seen on this harlequin* (Rasbora heteromorpha), *will respond to prompt treatment of the whole tank with a commercially available aquarium remedy.*

Fin rot

This problem is typical of poorly maintained tanks. It shows itself as a degeneration of the fin membranes, so that the fin rays stick out and the fins may look sore and inflamed. If caught early, a simple water change and overhaul of the filter system to restore its efficiency will rectify the problem. In more advanced cases, spot-treat, or treat the whole tank with an aquarium bactericide, depending on how many fish are affected.

Degeneration and erosion of barbels

There are two causes for this condition: poor water conditions and the use of a sharp substrate. If your fish have barbels and you have an outbreak of fin rot, the chances are that the barbels will degenerate to the point where parts of them break off. Treat as for fin rot described above. If the cause is erosion, the only solution is to change the substrate. The delicate barbels on catfish and loaches can be cut by sharp grains of gravel or sand, and secondary fungal and bacterial infections can then set in.

Split fins

If there is a lot of bickering going on in the tank, split or torn fins are a likely outcome. You may see one or two simple splits or completely ragged fins. Watch to see which fish is the culprit and remove it. If the victim is fit and well, the fins normally heal them-selves, but look for any signs of secondary infections from fungus or bacteria and treat as necessary.

Other problems

Occasionally you will get an unexplained death. This can happen even if you have been keeping fish for many years. If the other fish are fit and well, there is always the possibility that the fish died of old age.

Spotting fin rot

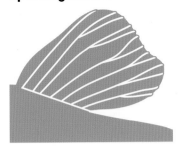

Become familiar with the shape of your fish's fins. They are normally smooth around the edge, although some may be naturally scalloped.

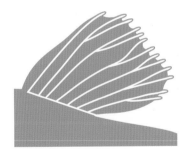

In poor conditions, the membrane between the fin rays degenerates, leaving the rays sticking out.

Right: *If left untreated, fin rot can spread to the body of the fish and weaken it to the point where it does not respond to treatment and dies. Treat all diseases promptly.*

To keep your fish and plants healthy in the closed system of an aquarium, you need to carry out regular maintenance. This should not be too time-consuming – an hour or so once a week will usually suffice. You'll need to carry out some maintenance tasks every day, others every two weeks, some monthly, and others less frequently. These times are only a guide, since each individual tank will vary depending on its size, method of filtration, and number of fish you keep.

By noting all your actions in an aquarium log, you will soon see a pattern developing that is right for your tank. Should something occur at the wrong time, you can refer back to see what has changed and you might have the answer to your problem.

Checking the temperature and health of your fish will become automatic when you pass the tank. Just brush your hand against the glass and get used to the feel of the tank at the right temperature. Get used to seeing how your fish behave and you will learn to notice slight alterations that indicate that there may be a problem on the way.

Water changes

Your first major maintenance task will be a water change and the purpose of this is to reduce the nitrates that can build up in the tank. (See page 26 for an explanation of how nitrates build up in the aquarium.) For this you need a bucket (it is best to keep one specifically for aquarium use), a length of siphon tubing (clear plastic is best because you can see if you inadvertently suck up something you shouldn't), and a siphon starter so that you don't get a mouthful of tank water when sucking on the tube to start it. Place the bucket on the floor, place one end of the tube in the tank, and start your siphon. Watch that you do not suck up any fish and also try to avoid spraying the water over your feet!

Right: This device enables you to clean the gravel and carry out a water change. Take care not to add too much tap water to the aquarium when using this device.

Left: Do not be tempted to put off or even omit water changes. Healthy water is the key to healthy fish, such as these flame tetras.

The tap pump connects to most tap fittings and can either create suction to clean the tank or allow water to pass through to fill the tank.

Push the tube into the gravel. Dirt and gravel swirl inside the tube, and the lighter debris is drawn off by siphon action.

A flow adjuster controls the speed of filling and/or cleaning. Keep it free of debris.

The flexible hose (shortened here) takes water to and from the aquarium.

Safety first

Before you start any work on your aquarium, turn off the electricity supply and unplug it, just in case someone switches it back on by mistake. Never work on your tank with the electricity switched on.

Testing the nitrite level

Keeping track of the nitrite levels in the tank is a worthwhile exercise. Test kits are quite easy to use. Always use a clean, dry vial so that the sample is not contaminated. Nitrite levels will fluctuate slightly and will certainly vary before and after a water change. After the initial peak during maturation, they should be negligible, but may rise when you have cleaned your filter because you have flushed away some of the beneficial bacteria and these will take a little time to build up again. Reducing feeding at this time to ease the load on the filter will help.

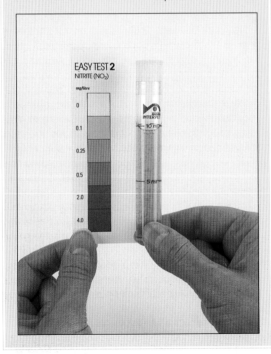

Left: *Regularly remove all debris from the gravel; noxious bacteria from decomposing organic material can cause problems with bottom-dwelling fish, such as these peppered Corydoras.*

When you get used to it, you will be able to suck up all the mulm (organic debris) on the substrate as you do your water change, thus doing two jobs at once. Take out 10-20% of the water. Before you throw the water away, check to make sure there are no life forms in it – you wouldn't be the first person to throw a fish out with the tank water!

While the water level is down, trim the plants by removing any dead or badly damaged leaves. You can also clean the front glass with an algae magnet or scraper to remove any algal growth.

Top up the tank with fresh water at the right temperature, either by siphoning it into the tank or by gently pouring it in with a pitcher. If you plan ahead, you can age this overnight and add a little boiled water to bring it back up to the right temperature. Or, you can add a water conditioner to remove any harmful chlorine. Spraying the water into the bucket before transferring it to the tank will also help get rid of the chlorine. Before replacing the condensation tray or cover glass, check that it is clean. Remove any buildup of salts from the water or algal growth so that it doesn't cut down the amount of light available to the plants.

Cleaning filters

Cleaning filters is a necessary evil when you keep fish. Filters should smell organic – a good earthy smell that is richer than when you take the condensation tray or cover glass off the tank. If the filters have a foul, putrid odor, they are not working properly and you need to find out why. Fortunately, this only happens if the air supply or water flow has been disrupted for several hours, preventing oxygen from reaching the filter media. After this time, the "good" (aerobic) bacteria have begun to die and the "bad" (anaerobic) bacteria have started to colonize the media. For this reason, you should never turn off your filter system for any longer than the time it takes to service it.

When cleaning a filter, always use clean, warm water at about the same temperature as that in the aquarium, or you risk killing off all the bacteria living in the filter medium. And, for the same reason, never use any detergents.

Internal power filters

The sequence of cleaning an internal power filter is shown in the photographs on these pages.

External power filters

The exact sequence of events will be dictated by the type of filter you have, but generally speaking, this is what you should do. Disconnect all the pipes. This may mean turning off the taps and uncoupling the joints, or it may mean taking all the pipework from the tank and carrying the filter to the sink. Remove the motor from the canister and clean any impellers. It is essential that these are free of debris. Wipe any slime from all the plastic parts. Remove the media from the canister. Some filters have modules that slide out, others have a single basket arrangement, while some models simply have a plate at the base to allow free passage of water in, then the media, and a plate at the top to prevent the media from getting into the motor. Clean what can be cleaned by rinsing in warm water. This includes porous tubes, slightly dirty filter floss and sponges, etc., to retain the bulk of the bacteria. Wipe clean all the plastic surfaces of the containers.

Reassemble the filter with fresh media as required. Check tubes to and from the aquarium to ensure that they are free of algae and there is no debris trapped in them; if need be, clean them with brushes suitable for the purpose.

1 Carefully remove the internal power filter from its supporting cradle and lift it from the tank without any debris falling back into the aquarium. It is a good idea to have a bowl or bucket ready to put it in, as it saves leaving a trail of dripping water all the way to the sink.

2 Over a bowl, bucket, or other receptacle, carefully separate the motor from the canister. You can place the canister in the bowl while you deal with the motor.

4 Remove the sponge from the canister and rinse it in clean, warm water to remove all the fine debris. Take out any other parts, such as screens and dividers, and wipe them clean. Clean the canister and external power filters on pages 44 and 47 in the same way.

5 Once you have finished cleaning all the parts, reassemble the filter and put it back in the tank. Make sure it is still working properly.

Useful spares

Make sure that you have the following spares available at all times, and remember to replace the ones you use.

Heater-thermostat
Suction cups
Diaphragms and filter
    pads for air pumps
Bearings, impeller, and
    O-ring seals for filters
Filter floss and/or
    sponges
Other media if used
Activated carbon
Thermometer
Nets
Fuses
Battery-operated
    air pump and batteries
    (do not keep them in
    the pump but with it)
Air line
Airstones
Starter for the lights

3 Clean any filter pads and impellers that may have become clogged with dirt and wipe off any slime on the plastic. Check the bearings and replace them if necessary.

Maintenance timetable

Daily
Remove uneaten food
Check temperature
Check that equipment
(filters, air pumps, lights)
is functioning properly
Check fish

Every 7-14 days
Partial water change
Remove dead vegetation
Remove debris from
substrate
Clean condensation
tray or cover glass
Clean front aquarium
glass to remove algae

Monthly
Clean filter
Vacuum-clean the gravel

Every 6-12 months
Service air pump
Service filter motor
Replace lighting
tubes

Several designs of gravel cleaner are available. This battery-powered unit is easy to use, as it has no trailing air line or cables to get in the way.

Undergravel filters

If an undergravel filter becomes clogged with dirt and debris, you will need to remove it completely from the tank to clean it properly. However, you can service an undergravel filter plate on a regular basis by using one of the many implements available to "vacuum-clean" the substrate. Either air- or battery-operated, these devices draw water and the surface layer of the gravel up a transparent tube. At a certain height the gravel falls back to the substrate under the force of gravity, and the water and debris continue through the device, where the dirt is trapped in a bag or plastic mesh compartment while the water flows through and back to the aquarium. Do not mix up all the substrate; if you disturb the entire filter bed, it will take some time for the useful bacteria to build up again. Just agitate the top layer to release most of the debris. You can also clean the undergravel filter bed when carrying out a water change (see page 70), but be careful not to siphon out the sand or gravel.

Left: *Algae magnets are available in several sizes. They are an easy, convenient, and efficient way of cleaning the inside of the tank glass without getting your hands wet.*

Air-operated box filters

Remove air-operated internal box filters from the aquarium and discard the dirtiest portion of the filter floss. Replace it with a fresh supply. Wash slightly soiled floss and reuse it – it has bacteria in it – and you can also wash and reuse the carbon.

Air pumps

Service air pumps regularly. The intake has a small filter pad, which can become clogged, reducing the pump's efficiency. The constant vibration of the diaphragm causes it to wear out and if this happens, your pump ceases to function. Check the manufacturer's instructions and replace both the filter pad and diaphragm regularly.

Heater-thermostats

Heater-thermostats require no regular maintenance; they either work or they don't. Keep a spare just in case your unit fails. A spare is also useful for emergencies, such as setting up a quarantine or breeding tank.

Aquarium lights

Although lights seem to go on forever, their useful output diminishes over time. It is worth replacing the tubes every 12 months to ensure good plant growth. You'll be surprised what a difference a new tube can make! The starter unit needs no maintenance but do check that the end caps have not decayed or the wires have not worn by rubbing against the edge of the hood. It is also a good idea to keep a spare starter in case this should fail.

Keeping your aquarium running smoothly

Replace the lighting tubes every 6-12 months.

Clean the condensation tray or cover glass every 7-14 days.

Do a partial water change every 7-14 days.

Check equipment such as filters, air pumps, heaters, and lights every day to make sure they are functioning properly.

Clean the filter every month.

Clean the front aquarium glass every 7-14 days to remove algae.

Service the filter motor every 6-12 months.

Remove dead vegetation every 7-14 days.

Check the temperature every day.

Check the fish every day.

Remove uneaten food every day.

Remove debris from the substrate every 7-14 days.

Vacuum-clean the gravel every month.

INDEX

Page numbers in **bold** indicate major entries; *italics* refer to captions and annotations; plain type indicates other text entries.

A

Acidity 12
Air lines 9, 46, 73
Air pump 47, *47*, 73, 74, 75
  diaphragm 47, 73
  filter pads 47
  piston 47
Airstone 24, 27, 46, 73
Algae 57
  as food 59, 61, 65
  magnet 71, 74
  scraper 71
Alkalinity 12
Amazon swordplant 30, 32, 51, 52, *52*
  planting **33**
  ruffled 51
Ammonia *26*
Ancistrus sp. 20
Anubias nana 51
Aquarium, planting the **28-33**

B

Bacopa 28
  caroliniana 50
  sp. 30
Bacteria 26
Barbs 56, 57, 62, *66*
Barbus
  conchonius 56
  tetrazona 6
  ticto 57
  titteya 56, 65
Blue gourami *60*
Brachydanio rerio 58
Breeding **64-65**
Bristlenose catfish 20
Bronze *Corydoras 61*

C

Cabinet 8, 10, 12, 13, 45
  ready-made *9*, 12
  unassembled *9*, 12
Cables 9
  filter 16
Cabomba
  caroliniana 51
  planting **31**
  sp. 30, *30*, 51
Catfish 61, 69
Cats 27
Ceratopsis thalictroides 51
Cherry barbs 26, *56*, 65
Children 10, 12, 18, 27, 49, *49*
Coolie loach *58*
Corydoras
  aeneus 61
  rabauti 68
Cryptocoryne 28, 32, 33,
  52, 52
  ciliata 51
  nevillii 51
  wendtii 51
  sp. 30, 51

D

Diseases
  degeneration of barbels 69
  fin rot 69, *69*
  fungus 67, 68, *68*
  split fins 69
  white spot 67, 68, *68*

E

Echinodorus
  major 51
  paniculatus 51, *52*
  tenellus 32, 51
Egg-layers 62, 64, 65

F

Feeding **62-63** *(See also* Food)
Filters **16-17**, 23, 26, 27, 28, 31, 38, **44-47**
  activated carbon 16
  air-operated 43
    box 74
  box 47, *47*
  cleaning 71
  floss 43, *44*, 73
  hangover *47*
  medium 16
  pipes 9
  plates 14
  power 16, 18
  external 9, **44-45**, *72*
    activated carbon *44*
    biological 45
    floss *44*
    inlet pipes *45*
    intake basket *45*
    internal canister *44*, 45
    mechanical 45
    media *44*
      foam pad *44*
      limestone chips *44*
      peat *44*
    porous pellets *44*
    outlet pipes *45*
    plastic barrel *44*
    pump motor housing *44*
    suckers *45*
    taps *45*
  internal **16-17**, *21*, 43, *72, 72*
    activated carbon 16
    foam cartridge *16*
    pump 17
      submersible *16*
    suction cups 17
    venturi effect 16
  sponge 39, 73
  suction cups 73
  undergravel 15, 45, 46, *46*, 47, *74, 74*
    plates 46
Fish health **66-69**, 70
Food *41*, 56, 58, **62-63**
  algae 65
  bloodworm 56, 57
  brine shrimp 65
    eggs 65
  daphnia 63
  dried *62*, 63
  flake 57, 59, 61, *62*, 63
  floating food sticks *62*
  freeze-dried *62*
    mosquito larvae *62*, 63
    tubifex *62*
  frozen 58, 60, 61, *62*, 63
    bloodworm *62*, 63
    chopped mussel *62*
    daphnia 56, 57
    peas *63*, 65
    shrimp *62*
  green foods 57, 58, 59, 61
  infusoria 65
  lettuce 63, *63*, 65
  liquid fry *62*
  live 58, 60, 63
  potato *63*
  powdered *62*
  sinking granules *62*
  tablet 61, *62*, 63
  water fleas *63*
  zucchini *63*
Flame tetras *70*

G

Giant ambulia 51
Guppies 43

H

Harlequin *68*
Heater
  installing **19**
  submersible heater-thermostat 18, *18*, *19*, *21*, 26, 27
  undertank heating mat 18
  suction cups 19, *19*
  thermometer 73
  thermostat 73, 74
    external 18
    internal 18
Heating **18-19**, 75
Helostoma temmincki 61
Hood 8, 9, 41, *41*
  cable ties 35
  fitting 36, **37**
  flying wires *34, 35*
  integral 8, 34
  lighting **35**, *39*
    clips *34, 35*
    fluorescent tubes *34*
    installing **35**
  preparing **34**
Hygrophila 30
  giant 51
  polysperma 51
  salicifolia 51
  willow leaf 51

I

Ichthyophthirius multifiliis 68
Insulation tape 13

J

Java fern 51, *53*
Java moss 51

K

Kissing gourami *61*
  green 61
  pink 61

L

Lighting
  fluorescent tube *34, 34*
    fitting *34, 34*
  units 9
Limnophila aquatica 51
Live-bearers 59, 62, 64
Loaches 69
Ludwigia
  mullertii 51
  palustris 51
  red 51
  repens 51
  sp. 30, *33*, *50*, 51

M

Maintenance **70-75**
Microsorium pteropus 51
Moonlight gourami *42*
Mulm 71

N

Neon tetras *4*
Nomaphila stricta 51

O

Oxygen levels 27

P

Pangio kuhlii 58
Paracheirodon innesi 4
Pearl gourami *60*
Peppered *Corydoras 71*
Pets 12
Plants 18
See also individual plant
  names
  aquatic 28
  basket 32
  before adding **26**
  choosing 32
  cuttings 30, 50
  fabric 55
  planting **28-33**
  plastic 50, **54-55**
  selection of **50-54**
Platies 26, *59*, 64
Power cuts 18
Pygmy chain swordplant 32

R

Rasbora heteromorpha 68
Rocks 10, *22*
  choosing and cleaning **22**
  granite *22*
  limestone 22, 24, 44
  pebbles *23*, 33
  placing **23**
  slate *22*
  tufa 22

weathered 22, *22*
Rosy barb *56*
  long-finned form 56
Rotala indica 51

S

Silicone aquarium sealer 8, 13,
  20, 22
Stand *8*, 10, *10*, *12*, 13
  choosing **8-9**
  setting up 12
Substrates 75
  choosing and preparing **14**
  gravel 10, 14, *15*, *25*, *29*
    black *14*
    cleaner 74, *74*
    coarse *14*
    colored 14, *14*
    fine *14*
    medium *14*
  natural sand (river) 14, *14*
  streambed 14
Swordtails 26, *59*
Synnema triflorum 50, 51

T

Tanichthys albonubes 57
Tank
  acrylic 8
  background
    choosing **38**
    neutral *38*
    plant scenes *38*
    plastic 38
    rockwork *38*
    sunken cities *38*
    trees and logs 38
  breeding 46, 47, 66

capacities 9
choosing **8-9**
cleaning and leveling **13**
condensation tray 9, 27, 37, *39*,
  41
  fitting **36**
decoration 48, *48*, 49, *49*
filling **25**
furnished, with fish **41**
glass *12*, 23, *45*
hygiene 25
installing **12**
  checklist 12
maturing 38, *39*
placing **10-11**
power outages 18
quarantine 46, 47, 66, 67
secondhand 9
size 9, 12, 70
temperature 12, 18, 26
Ticto barb *57*
Tiger barb *6*
Trichogaster
  gold form *60*
  leeri 60
  microlepis 42
  opaline form 60
  trichopterus 60
Tropical fish 18, 24
  adding **40**
  selection of **56-61**
Two-spot barb *57*

V

Vallis 52
  straight 51, 52, *52*
  twisted 51, 52, *52*
Vallisneria 28, *31*
  planting **29**

spiralis 30, 51
tortifolia 51
Vine roots 20

W

Water
  acidic 24, 25, 56
  adding **24**
  alkaline 24, 25, 56
  ammonia 45
  changes 70
  chemistry 22, 24, 40
  conditioner 71
  degrees of hardness (°dH) 24
  filling the tank **25**
  flow 44
  hard 24, 44, 56
  hardness 22, 24
  level 27, 29
  nitrates 24, 26, *26*, 28
  nitrites 26, *26*, 45, 71, *71*
  nitrogen cycle 16, 26
  phosphates *24*
  pH scale *12*, 25
    test kits 25
    electronic meters 25
  pollution control 24
  quality 56
  running in the system **26**
  soft 24, 44, 56
  switching on the system **27**
  tap 24
  thermometer 26, 38, *38*, *39*,
    40, *41*, 56, 57
Water wisteria 30, *50*, 51
Whiptail catfish *65*
White Cloud Mountain
  minnow 26, *57*
Wood *33*

adding **21**
bogwood 20, *20*
choosing and preparing **20**
cork 20
  tiles 20
mopani 20, *20*
natural 21

X

Xiphophorus
  helleri 59
  maculatus 59

Z

Zebra danio *58*

CREDITS

The majority of the photographs featured in this book have been taken by Geoffrey Rogers and are © Interpet Publishing.

The publishers would like to thank the following photographers for providing images, credited here by page number and position: B(Bottom), T(Top), C(Center), BL(Bottom Left), etc.

David Allison: 56(BL)
MP & C Piednoir/Aqua Press - France: Copyright page, 42, 57(L), 58(B), 59(TR,B), 61(BL), 65(T), 70(BL)
Hans Georg Evers: 61(TR)
Photomax (Max Gibbs): 56(T), 58(T), 60(BR), 64, 68(TR,B), 71(T)
Mike Sandford: 24, 49(TL,BR), 51(TC), 60(TL), 63(BL,C), 65(B), 69
Iggy Tavares: 57(CR), 66
W A Tomey: Title page, 6

The artwork illustrations have been prepared by Stuart Watkinson and are © Interpet Publishing.

Thanks are due to Dorking Aquatics, Dorking, Surrey, England; Eheim GmbH & Co Kg, D-73779, Deizisau, Germany; Heaver Tropics; Ash, Sevenoaks, Kent, England; John Allan Aquariums Ltd., Bury St Edmunds, Suffolk England; Morden Water World, Surrey; England; Swallows Aquatics, Millbrook Garden Centre, Southfleet, Kent, England; Tetra Second Nature, Blacksburg, VA 24060-6671, USA; and Woodland Nurseries Garden Centre, West Kingsdown, Kent, England, for their help during the preparation of this book.